THE CHALLENGE OF
BEING HUMAN

THE CHALLENGE OF BEING HUMAN

Michael Eigen

Routledge
Taylor & Francis Group
LONDON AND NEW YORK

First published 2018
by Routledge
2 Park Square, Milton Park, Abingdon, Oxon OX14 4RN

and by Routledge
711 Third Avenue, New York, NY 10017

Routledge is an imprint of the Taylor & Francis Group, an informa business

© 2018 Michael Eigen

The right of Michael Eigen to be identified as the author of this work has been asserted in accordance with sections 77 and 78 of the Copyright, Designs and Patents Act 1988.

All rights reserved. No part of this book may be reprinted or reproduced or utilised in any form or by any electronic, mechanical, or other means, now known or hereafter invented, including photocopying and recording, or in any information storage or retrieval system, without permission in writing from the publishers.

Trademark notice: Product or corporate names may be trademarks or registered trademarks, and are used only for identification and explanation without intent to infringe.

British Library Cataloguing-in-Publication Data
A catalogue record for this book is available from the British Library

Library of Congress Cataloging-in-Publication Data
A catalog record has been requested for this book

ISBN: 978-1-78220-653-8 (pbk)

Typeset in Palatino
by The Studio Publishing Services Ltd
email: studio@publishingservicesuk.co.uk

CONTENTS

ABOUT THE AUTHOR   vii

PREFACE   ix

CHAPTER ONE
Alternate infinities   1

CHAPTER TWO
Psychopathy in everyday life   11

CHAPTER THREE
Image, fullness, void   25

CHAPTER FOUR
Where are we going?   37

CHAPTER FIVE
Thinking about squirrels   47

CHAPTER SIX
O, orgasm, and beyond   59

CHAPTER SEVEN
Just beginning: ethics of the unknown   71

CHAPTER EIGHT
Life kills, aliveness kills   77

CHAPTER NINE
Mini-moments   81

CHAPTER TEN
Leaving and the impossible place   93

CHAPTER ELEVEN
Giving it a try   107

CHAPTER TWELVE
Affect images and states   121

CHAPTER THIRTEEN
Everything human; hidden sprouts and psyche talk   127

REFERENCES   139

INDEX   143

ABOUT THE AUTHOR

Michael Eigen worked with disturbed, especially psychotic, children in his twenties, then adults in his thirties and onwards. He directed an institute program for working with creative individuals at the Center for Psychoanalytic Training and was the first Director of Educational Training at the Institute for Expressive Analysis. He was on the Board of Directors at the National Psychological Association for Psychoanalysis for eight years, first as Program Chair, then editor of *The Psychoanalytic Review*. He has taught at many institutes and colleges and has given talks and seminars internationally. In the past twenty years, he taught and supervised mainly at the National Psychological Association for Psychoanalysis and the New York University Postdoctoral Program in Psychotherapy and Psychoanalysis. He gives a private seminar on Winnicott, Bion, Lacan, and his own work, ongoing nearly forty years. *The Challenge of Being Human* is his twenty-sixth book.

PREFACE

The challenge of being human faces us throughout our lives, a never-ending challenge individually and communally. What to do with the many tendencies that create and live us and we live, capacities that lift us to unimaginable places and cast us down to nameless horrors?

Freud wrote that the greatest problem facing humanity is its destructive urge. There are many approaches to working with, channeling, controlling, taming, modulating, transcending–subtending, using the aggressive force that has played an important role in survival and evolution. All our tendencies have come in handy in one or another moment. Much has been written on hypertrophy of one or another tendency and misfit or mistimed matching of capacity to context. So much of life is trial and error, experimental as well as habitual, unending modulating inner–outer possibilities. How we get along with ourselves, each other, and worlds we live in can be a life and death matter and, at other times, a question of experiential enrichment.

Issues of becoming human have been noted since antiquity. Biblical prophets spoke of a circumcision of the heart, turning a heart of stone to heart of flesh. He without sin among you cast the first stone. Saint Paul: God is love. Saint Augustine: Love and do as you will. And yet destruction continues. Near the end of their lives, Moses and Freud wondered which will win, goodness or destructiveness? If we are part of a universe, as scientists say, that began with an explosion, it is not farfetched to imagine we, too, are partly explosive.

Studies link violence with social and economic deprivation. Yet, there are ways the violence that harms most comes from high places, people of wealth and position, where power of a few affects lives of many. There is no one factor that solves the issue. We live in a universe with many moods, tendencies, forces, coloration. Moments of peace and war seem part of the makeup of physical, biological, spiritual processes. Ancients wrote about creative–destructive war between elements, something Freud tuned into, as he depicted tensions between human capacities.

This book explores the work of many tendencies that make us up and capacities that try to meet them. Growth of capacity to tolerate and work with experience is a major theme of depth psychologies as well as many other approaches that attempt to partner our capacities with less injury.

Chapter One, "Alternate infinities," explores a theme introduced in *The Psychotic Core*, the need for infinities to add to and qualify each other. It is as if, among our capacities, is a kind of free-floating sense of infinity. Almost anything can be infinitized. William Blake sees infinity in a grain of sand, Levinas in the human face. Many kinds of infinities in many kinds of situations, partly depending on affective attitude, impact, and vision.

Common sense puts the brakes on, looks at things from many angles, takes into account multiple dimensions and viewpoints. Yet, too often, it is unable to prevent murder. There are moments when infinities feed murder. Warring infinities, murderous infinities. My infinity is better than yours, mine truth, yours false. Yes, survival feeds murder, too, property, possession, scarcity–abundance, food, and procreation. We live in so many dimensions at once, it is no wonder we try to simplify and reduce our experiential maps to get along. If only we would get along.

Some note it could be worse. We feel murder so keenly because it is not the norm and are horrified (and sometimes relieved) when some try to make it the norm. We are paradoxical beings and when infinity meets obdurate realities, it may try to annihilate the latter or *vice versa*. Usually, we try to solve problems, work with them, or give up for a time and let them be, move on to another part of existence. We learn at an early age that detours and alternatives are possible. But attempts to rid ourselves of problems by murder is part of our repertoire. The Biblical God, too, often models this possibility for us. As we repeatedly discover, work with multiple capacities in multiple ways is part of our evolutionary challenge.

Chapter Two, "The psychopathy of everyday life," brings out multiple functions of psychopathic tendencies, including its work in political and economic processes today. It was finished a few months before the November, 2016 election and includes a section related to Trump, his brother, and the current situation. I am grateful to *The Psychoanalytic Review* for its rapid publication (2016, Volume 103, Number 6, pp. 729–742). It is reprinted with permission of the National Psychological Association for Psychoanalysis. Therapeutic work with psychopathic tendencies is a challenge that requires profound engagement.

Chapter Three, "Image, fullness, void", is reprinted from *Psychoanalytic Inquiry*, 2016, Volume 36, Number 18, pp. 613–619. It honors the complex work of image, long a second-class citizen in epistemology. Its work has always been acknowledged by poets and mystics and plays a major role in psychoanalysis. In addition to image, this chapter traces links between experiences of fullness–void so often treated as antitheses. Many capacities feed each other. How we relate to them plays a role in ways potential tensions are experienced.

Chapter Four, "Where are we going?" is based on a graduation talk I gave at The National Psychological Association for Psychoanalysis, December 16, 2016. I have included two earlier graduation talks in Chapter Twelve. I collected theses talks here because I think what is said to students graduating from psychoanalytic programs says something essential about our field and time. They are more than emblems of a particular field. They probe the psyche of moment, areas germane to our lives today, individually and communally. As citizens of humanity, personal and world challenges interweave.

Chapter Five, "Thinking about squirrels", amplifies material I gave at recent talks for The National Psychological Association for Psycho-analysis, Das Unbehagen, Hearing Voices NYC, and the United States Chapter of the International Society for Psychological and Social Approaches to Psychosis. This chapter brings out different responses to impossible situations, ways of approaching limits of our personalities and ways we feel trapped by our environment. After discussing ways animals respond to a trap or difficult problem, we delineate a child's response to learning about his father's oncoming death, a woman's response to discovering meaninglessness, and pathways Schreber opened for us through his psychosis. Here, we touch not only ways we respond to difficulty, but situations that seem impossible, the problem of psychological birth and forces against it.

Chapter Six, "O, orgasm, and beyond" appeared in *Psychoanalytic Dialogues*, 2015, Volume 25, Number 5, pp. 646–654. Vast numbers of dimensions characterize life experience, among them orgasmic dimensions. This chapter explores aspects of orgasmic life as well as movements that transcend, subtend, go beyond orgasm, and, perhaps, O, Bion's term for ultimate reality. There are ways we go deeper than ourselves, touching something nameless that gives life profound, inexpressible meaning. It may be that Bion's O and Buddhist "ultimate reality" have something in common, yet do not exhaust the nameless mystery informing (in-forming) us.

A version of Chapter Seven, "Just beginning: ethics of the unknown," was published in *New Therapist*, 2015, Number 100. Beginning never stops. If we take that seriously, deeply, we begin to undergo an ethical transformation as well as other changes. The unknown is felt as a partner in the creativity of our lives and meeting with others. A deeper respect for what we do not or cannot know underlies what we do and can know. Bion reaches for the term "Faith" to portray the growth of a psychoanalytic attitude, openness to the unknown emotion of moment. Rather than static, our approach to experience is ever in process, a humble, caring part of our beings. Bion humorously calls this part of the human challenge "humbly dumbly" in *A Memoir of the Future*, humbly bumbling along, singing our songs, *Memoir* one of Bion's songs growing from the music of his life, bumbling and bumping along. I think of Ray Bradbury's *Farenheit 451*, where people became books to preserve expressiveness as well as knowledge. We can, too, feel the songs of our lives, music felt by ourselves and others. And, by a miracle of culture, songs, books, and artifacts from thousands of years ago become part of our expressive beings we pass on to others, transmission of what we feel most deeply but may not be able to say. "What did Job see too wonderful to say?" Yet we feel it, share it.

Chapter Eight, "Life kills, aliveness kills" was published in *New Therapist*, 2012, Number 76. We are up against ourselves. To live, we kill. Aliveness kills. It is not just an aberration, a result of bad upbringing and conditions. It is part of life. Yet, our sensitivity recoils at this seeming necessity. We would like to change this, stop it, do something better.

Our economic system is fused with the taste of power and feeds on its own ambition. Yet, pointing to external conditions is not enough without also working with our psychological bent. We are challenged by our own nature and proclivities and necessities. Something in us goes beyond them, eggs us further. We insist we are not done evolving, growing, learning, feeling, caring. In this chapter, I list eight aspects of our makeup that play a role in destructiveness, an open invitation to face ourselves and see what we can do, where we can go. We have not yet plumbed all our resources; we have not exhausted our possibilities.

Chapter Nine, "Mini-moments," is based on five vignettes published by the Newsletter of the International Society for Psychological and Social Approaches to Psychosis (ISPS-US). They depict interactions in sessions with five different patients struggling with psychosis. In time, each became hospital free and continued working at the edge of their beings. The sessions shared occurred and were published over a nine year period: "Marin and I" (2007), "Impenetrable shatter" (2010), "Where is your face?" (2010), "Voice echoes" (2011), and "Every morning" (2016). There is a hunger for affective imagination that touches nerves aching for contact, often deep in graveyards of personality. Whatever barriers and challenges psychosis presents, there is also opportunity for speaking behind one's back from places one did not know or see, which pass from heart to heart, mind to mind. Often, loss and damage are parts of it, but also finding of moments that make a difference.

Chapter Ten, "Leaving and the impossible place," follows tributaries of one of the most important experiences of life, loss and leaving. Going towards and away from another and oneself is one of the basic dual movements in our lives. Norm is deeply married with all its ups and downs, yet entertains a possible affair with one of his former patients, Denise, who offers fantasy gratification, the gratification–frustration his marriage lacks. To complicate the difficulty, Denise has a chronic problem, leaving once a connection becomes too real. Closeness is all right as long as closeness is not too close. Once a relationship becomes demanding, with hurdles to meet, she goes her single way. So often people reach an impossible place. I would like to posit the impossible place with thousands of faces. Its form changes, but a sense of unsolvable impasse or dilemma is a kind of constant.

I like to think of Boddhidharma meditating in front of a wall for nine years. I feel it as a wall inside of us that, one way or other, we all share, walls of personality. If we sit with our walls the latter might or might not change, but we do. We change through the very activity of sitting with walls, an important kind of growing. We might not "solve" the impossible place, but we can make good use of it in our own development. Not simply banging our heads against it like squirrels in Chapter Five, but developing new forms of relationship, including ways of approach and approach-avoidance.

Lou, the second patient focused on in this chapter, severed his life with severe judgment. A kind of fusion–oscillation of judgment-void, in which judgment became a kind of relationship and leaving became a form of staying. Our amazing psyche can leave by staying and stay by leaving. Towards–away, plenitude–loss form many combinations. Lou was baffled by his own sensitivity and shock of himself. As I write at the end of the chapter, "The shock of ourselves is perennial. We are challenged by our own aliveness."

Chapter Eleven, "Giving it a try," is mostly made up of dialogue between Gerry and me. Gerry suffered devastating psychotic states and underwent hospitalizations for his own protection. In this chapter, we meet him well into process of working in therapy, no longer needing hospitalization. He is dedicated to trying to stay with, and communicate, momentary states, letting affective imagination grow. Therapy provides a relatively safe place to let this kind of exploration happen.

I share some of my thoughts and responses with the reader and Gerry, but in much of the chapter I let the dialogue and interactions speak for themselves, an adventure in mutual sensitivity and possibility. Bad feeling persists, but a good thread also appears, its impact appreciated. Tolerance and desire for rich interweaving grows.

Chapter Twelve, "Affect images and states," was written for *the Journal of Humanistic Psychology*, scheduled to be online and in paper edition in 2018. It is used here by permission. It provides an informal background for working with affective images and states as part of therapeutic movement. Some workers mentioned include Freud, Jung, Elkin, Bion, Winnicott, Lacan, Bettelheim, Arieti, and my own writings. You can see from this list the importance of psychotic experience in this work, its destructive–creative possibilities.

Don, the patient focused on in this chapter, is over-loaded with self-hate, frequently comparing himself with shit and worse. At the time of the writing, he has been hospital free for over ten years. The searing pain that threatens to blot him out has become a reality we can touch in sessions. Often, relief is found not by direct confrontation, but through patches of other kinds of experience. Both of us grow in appreciation of treasures within and between us, while aware the pain fire can arise anytime, along with the fecal self. Little by little, creativity became an important part of his life. This chapter details some of the processes Don went through and goes through as his difficult journey continues.

Chapter Thirteen. "Everything human, hidden sprouts and psyche talk," is based on two more graduation talks (Chapter Four is another). The first is "Everything human," for the National Psychological Association for Psychoanalysis, in 2010. The second, "Hidden sprouts and psyche talk," was for the New York University Postdoctoral Program in Psychotherapy and Psychoanalysis, 2007. What is said to graduating colleagues from psychoanalytic training institutes has dramatic importance, taking the temperature of depth psychology in our day, its health and relevance. The talks touch special contributions our work has made, is making, can make to the growth and well being of individuals and the greater social body.

The work of time

Our collective memory goes far into the past and future as beings of time. We are interested in what we were like before cities and farms, how we survived and got along. We try to learn as much as we can from remains we find and hints from communal living before the great building began. Building and exploring take many forms and use many capacities. Not only tools and homes, but images act as instrumental and expressive vehicles. We are thrilled and frightened by images we create and create us. We are driven by thirst for discovery on many fronts, incessantly egging us on, ideas and experiences as well as tangible materials. There is much loss and damage and wondrous gain.

The very act of breathing opens worlds, as does touch, sight, hearing, sensing in ways known and unknown. We write stories about life in the future as we worry about the present moment. Science and art are like arms and heart. So many accidents of meaning, art is in heart, and so is hear, ear, art as a form of heart hearing.

How do our capacities get along, how do *we* get along? This book does not supply answers, but it invites us to further taste ourselves. In earlier work (e.g., *The Sensitive Self*), I wrote of psychic taste buds. It challenges us to open doors. At this moment of history, we still do not know if we will ever get along without killing each other. The fact that we kill to live is far from digestible. Yet, we are living, creating, being, doing, wondering.

When I look around my seminar, I see amazing beings, so different from each other, yet engaged in search and caring. Do they hurt others and get hurt? Of course, indeed yes. It is impossible to live without injury. But do we have growing, if delicate, capacity to ameliorate injury to ourselves and others? Can we grow in taking in our situation in ways that potentially enrich? We are working on it, practicing, studying, doing what we can—and sometimes more, much more.

This book is an invitation to walk and work together in exploring the human challenge, the challenge of being human, inevitably partial and incomplete, touching walls and passages, part of inner quest and hope.

How do we get from here to there, or more deeply here? There is no end to here. Each moment has fathomless depths. We sense what we can with intimations of more. I am an eighty-two-year-old man who runs ten or so miles at a time and exchanges words and looks with many people wherever I run. The exchange happens spontaneously, momentary, without asking about political or religious beliefs or any questions that might divide–unite. And wherever I run, exchanges are very similar.

Stranger: How ya doin?
M. E.: Still here—happy to be here.
Stranger: [Big smile, thumbs up]—you said it bra, happy to be here.

The other evening, a slight variation, running with the most beautiful wide, high sunset and as I ran past people, all kinds of people, sitting by the boats, or a hill or pond or cemetery or lunch stand, I simply opened my arms and palms with a smile and said, "Beautiful." That is what my heart felt.

And *everyone* nodded, smiled, and said, "Beautiful," some in a whisper. That is what they were feeling in their hearts in this breath-giving sunset. How do we all get to and share this place in the power world? We have it in our hearts.

CHAPTER ONE

Alternate infinities

There is an area of self that is in heaven.
All terms in the above statement are suspect: area, self, in, heaven.

What can they mean? Yet, such a statement attempts to communicate a state of being, an experience. To make matters worse, an ancillary claim is that this state goes on unconsciously all the time: the kingdom of heaven is within you, not simply a matter of consciousness, but part of unconscious being, supporting, informing consciousness.

Self in heaven, heaven in self.

To be somewhat Freudian, it is akin to saying we are totally gratified all the time. "You open your hand and satisfy the desire of every living being," says the psalmist. Gratification total, pulsing, ongoing, whether or not we are aware of it.

We, also, are ever frustrated. It is as if two states exist simultaneously, inverse images of each other: total gratification, total frustration. At times, they feel mutually antagonistic, but they also fuse, become indistinguishable. Total gratification–total frustration: intertwined, persistent.

Mystics affirm an incorruptible point of soul in contact with God. Yet, our lived self is, to various degrees, corrupt, tainted, poisonous. How do both states exist together? We tend to pit one against the other, calling one real at the other's expense. But our capacity to generate contrasting experiences is real, as is our capacity to generate contrasting interpretations of any experience.

One may substitute "is" for "in": Self is heaven, heaven is self.

* * *

Bion (1994, p. 95) writes that every dream is a developmental failure. It tries at once to process and evade emotional impacts, to evacuate and metabolize emotional experience. The psyche tries to get rid of and process itself, to deflect and let in experience.

For anyone to be alive, murderous wishes must be frustrated. That you and I are alive together means we have survived our wish to kill each other and ourselves. Being alive is frustrating, insofar as aliveness escapes destruction. Destructiveness is part of aliveness, yet must compromise with the latter if aliveness is to survive itself. To be alive means that destructive urges towards self and other remain partially unsatisfied. This coheres with Freud's belief that psychic life requires repression/suppression, some sort of modulation.

As a group we commit a lot of murder. It is not clear that we can survive without destructiveness. Is destructiveness as part of aliveness a problem requiring solution or a fact requiring digestion? Some claim meditation on destructiveness helps to modify the latter or ourselves, even if destructiveness is part of survival. Awareness of destruction can spur evolution of self.

Bion feels our madness is such that we hallucinate total murder, successful obliteration of living soul, psyche, feeling, thinking. Emotional impacts obliterate us and we try to obliterate emotional impacts. Yet, and this is crucial, in some form we survive our feelings and they survive us. We deform each other, feeling continues, we continue. Murder does not have the only word.

Are we ever fully anything—alive or dead? We taste qualities/degrees of aliveness–deadness. We are partly destroyed beings throbbing with life. In madness, we lose ability to let one state qualify another. In truth we taste ourselves, taste again, noting differences, making comparisons, letting one state challenge, nourish another, speak together, interweave. We evolve capacity to feel our feelings, to appreciate our states, recognize contributions of competing capacities. If we must murder, at least sometimes let us murder smugness about murdering.

I think there are ways to feel murderousness through our bodies and beings, the power of it, the need of it, without actually killing. At first glance this seems a little like experiencing sexuality without having sex. Murder without actually murdering, sex without climax. But I do feel orgasmic power through my body and feeling being, the surge of it, fullness of it—without it becoming the act itself. Am I kidding myself, evolving?

Bion contrasts frustration modification with frustration evasion. In the latter, the psyche cannot tolerate itself, gets rid of itself, it cannot support its own tension. In the former an attempt is made to evolve the capacity to process feelings. If I were totally mad, I could totally evade awareness of frustration. But I also hunger for feelings, for contact with life.

* * *

The analyst is in a difficult position when confronted by a psychotic person. If he sides with the individual, the latter thinks him mad or irresponsible. If he sides with the group, the patient thinks him insensitive, uncaring. This is characteristic of the "can't win" element in many therapy situations.

The psychotic individual, or individual in states of psychosis, also appreciates signs of empathic responsiveness, even if wondering what is wrong with the person offering it. Who—unless devoid of common sense—would treat him as sane, valuable, ready for dialogue? At the same time, he might operate with a presumption of intimacy, assuming the other is interested in his thoughts, spilling all with a speed impossible to process, trying to create, find, convey a totality one cannot keep up with. It is an intimate warmth without recognition of the other's rights, the other's needs, smarting at the core with panic of being ostracized. He disdains and fears the group beyond him, threatened by incomprehension, brutality, neglect, unmeetable demands, unwanted help. In special moments, he feels threatened by feeling awareness.

The patient requires the analyst's devotion—to the patient, to his profession, the analyst's double-agency, playing one against the other, needing both. In downward spirals, fault lines widen and the analyst splits, caught between betrayal of the client and the group. The split is less between individual and impulse as between what Bion calls narcissism–socialism.

In one of his formulations, Freud emphasized conflict between individual and species (ego and sexual instincts). The species might not care about the fate of the individual and dupe the latter into reproductive acts that might not always be in the latter's interest. The competitive vision is that there are junctures where individual success might be at the species' expense and *vice versa*. The cooperative vision is that they contribute to each other's enrichment and possibility. Freud enjoys emphasizing one up–other down.

Bion emphasizes bipolarity. Sex and aggression are variably weighted on the side of the individual's fulfillment as an individual and group member. There are many ways groups call for the sacrifice of individuals and individuals react against group tyranny, but this does not cancel an essential symbiotic relationship between them. Sexual–aggressive impulses are organized through narcissistic–socialistic attitudes and needs, more harmoniously or conflictually (can there ever be totally conflict-free states?).

Individuals feel pressures to survive, to live, to live well, to sacrifice for the group, even give up life in time of war, mould to others. The interaction of factors is dizzyingly complex, since groups provide instruments for the individual's self-realization (viz., language for a writer, medical school and hospitals for surgeons, religion for worshippers, armies for fighters, governments for reformers or power hopefuls, etc.). We do what we can with materials at hand but there are casualties. Personalities buckle under pressure to fulfill themselves or even get by. Opposite poles of our being seek satisfaction, often at our expense. Our sensitivity registers pressures it must work with and we might attack our sensitivity rather than learn more about what we are experiencing. Building tolerance for conflictual experiencing is harder than obliterating sensitivity, but has its own rewards.

Summary of loose Bionic detour

1. The dream seeks to fulfill pleasure and reality principles and falls short. The pleasure principle seeks discharge of tensions, satisfaction of wishes, evasion of frustration. The reality principle

seeks frustration modification, problem solving, learning to work with pressures. Matters are complicated by each principle containing the other, each capable of tyranny or generosity. Overriding attitudes run through both, lending affective context and structure to how either functions. This is more than a Chinese box situation. It is a matter of spirit or struggle with spirits, tone, taste, and texture of being. It is as true to say the dream is often a partial success as well as failure. It is a nexus of sensations, feelings, perceptions, visions, intimations in which evasion and modification somewhat work together.

Underlying this account is a sense that pleasure and reality principles strive for maximum satisfaction. An unconscious sense of total satisfaction and frustration exist together, akin to saying orgasm and emptiness coincide.

2. Meanings and loci of sanity–madness shift. A psychotic individual's sensitivity might not be able to take group madness. Group morality can be cruel, its judgments murderous. But there are murderous individuals too, whether mad, psychopathic, or power driven. A therapist may cross the line to help an individual and look bad to his group, or fail to cross the line and look bad to his patient. It is an art to be uncaring in a caring way or caring in a way that maintains sufficient self-protectiveness.

Notions of narcissism–socialism arise from a common emotional substratum. Concepts emphasize various distributions of whatever binds–separates. Different notions of individuals and groups try to maximize themselves. We are challenged to keep up with voices living produces.

3. The link between sensitivity, rage, and murderousness is crucial. Murder–suicide promises total relief from sensitivity, indignity, injustice. It seems, too, a way to get what one wants, to blow away barriers. We have the ability to mask the boundless quality of rage by pinpointing targets.

Murder seeks a perfect solution, hallucinates totality. Whether orgasmic and/or calculating, it attempts to correct a troubling state without realization that it itself is part of the troubling state. Individuals or groups might win for a time, but humanity still has its murderousness to reckon with. Shakespeare insists murderers have nightmares. The problem of what to do with ourselves persists in trying to be without ourselves. Violence is too simple a tool to solve the problems consciousness produces.

Questions

Human consciousness–unconsciousness magnifies–minifies. It exaggerates, blows things up, depreciates. Bion notes we have a spontaneous tendency towards hyperbole. In some sense, we are natural liars.

Lying often tries to make felt truth noticeable, gaining attention by exaggeration. A difficulty is that attempts to attract attention might obfuscate what one is trying to call attention to. One might end up getting lost in lies, to the point that thinking warps, becomes poisonous. One no longer knows what one pays attention to and the effort to sort things out begins from scratch.

We thus have a strong urge to reach the zero or starting point, to see what really is there. We have a drive to push past our lying ways. We confront not just ignorance or illusion, but deception. We might even wonder if the drive for truth is our biggest deception of all. Pure truth: another hallucinatory totality. Nevertheless, study of ourselves continues.

* * *

States infinitize. William Blake: "All states are eternal." Freudian drives attract infinity. In *The Psychotic Core* (2004a) I wrote about infinities qualifying each other. It is not simply that infinity comes up against limits and must draw back. It meets other infinities and they wonder at each other, take each other in.

"Hey, he's God too!" says the teacher to the student who learned he was God, only to refuse to budge when a man on an elephant lumbered toward him.

Freud could not resist writing about psychic realities as gods or forces or characters from great works: Eros, Thanatos, Ananke. He sensed he was working with infinity filters. Concepts are a little like the magician who cuts up the lady in a sideshow, only to reveal she is whole before the main show begins. But these imaginary slices release energy, possibly create–destroy energy. Imagination is part of reality and is part of the way reality changes. To say imagination creates realities simply acknowledges that it is intrinsic to the way reality works.

In *The Electrified Tightrope* (2004b), I wrote of libido seeking an ideal imago. The intertwining of Freudian drives and ideal states (whether creative/destructive) is a vision of an imaginative body, life in which will, drives, and hallucinatory fantasy are indissolubly connected

To hallucinate perfection while in agony, a fulfilling breast when hungry, the drive creates, attracts, attacks ideal states. Not just any feed, a good feed, not just a good feed, a beatific one. Infinitely wonderful, infinitely horrible. Sexuality infinitizes love objects. Murder nullifies hate objects. Nullity can be a kind of negative infinity. Negative infinites multiply to keep up with the need to nullify hated realities. Intentions, spirits, attitudes create realities, since they *are* realities. Bion felt that destructive results of psychoanalysis are proof of the latter's power. The ideal of total destruction is very powerful and grows from a felt need, not just to wipe out a group or person, but to wipe out sensitivity. As long as sensitivity survives attempts to quell it, we will upset ourselves and others.

One imagines getting rid of the object gets rid of distress, only to discover sensitivity never lacks for objects.

What is Freud's heritage?: the ubiquity of hallucination in desire, the ubiquity of desire in human strivings. Madness runs through it.

Can we ever be sure we are not hallucinating? Perhaps a beginning is: we can be sure we are.

* * *

A practical question, an ethical one. When you make an assertion that might be costly to another person (injure sensitivity), think first, "How am I hallucinating? What truth am I hallucinating? What other am I hallucinating?" Nothing is a better index of hallucinatory murder than the sense of being right.

Yes, it is important to stick up for what you believe is right. You must fight for what you believe true, if necessary. But remember, as you do, those who have been maimed, tortured, extinguished in the name of truth and right.

One might not solve this knot but one can spend more time wondering.

In spite of realities of power politics and big business ("The Economic Age"), I think everyone should spend more time feeling. More time feeling feelings. Then look at other people.

Levinas writes (1969, 1987) of the infinite in the other's face. A sense of infinity that makes me feel the person through and through, uncompromiseable realness of the other, otherness of the other.

Although I may feel the other's realness, this does not mean I know the other. I cannot reduce another to knowledge. The other's otherness, realness, means he will be outside what I can know of him. I may learn this or that (know him like the back of my hand, used for slapping, caressing, grasping) but who the other is remains mysterious. I am obligated to guard the mystery of the other, to value the infinitely precious challenge whether or not fulfillable, heart to heart, face to face.

The infinite shines through the other's face. Not kingdom of heaven within. Perhaps not even heaven. Infinite call, reaching, caring. A life of approach. Quality of approach matters. Closeness part of distance, distance part of closeness.

Does this mean we hallucinate infinity, otherness, distance, closeness? Is there a menu of hallucinations we select from, which select us? It is said ego/self are hallucinatory: we hallucinate ourselves. Hallucinate ourselves hallucinating ourselves. We appreciate common sense, science, art, music, literature, alternate approaches to reality, ways reality realizes itself through us, as us. So many avenues of access lessen the posibility of being totally enslaved by any one. Alternate hallucinatory experiences qualify each other.

Reality hallucinates itself through us. If reality realizes, in part, through hallucination, it is an imaginative reality indeed. Hallucinatory imagination plays a role in the way life tastes.

What about people who claim to be prosaic, down to earth, dry, unimaginative practical people of action dealing with life as it is: do they negatively hallucination a life without hallucination? What dangerous tyranny can this breed, imagining oneself hallucination-free, scoffing at hallucinators.

We can no longer conceive or make sense of ourselves without dream-work.

Body, psyche, spirit pass through dreams. We are dream-woven beings in the kind of world that gives rise to dreaming, the kind of world that is altered by dreams. There are ways in which wishing can make it so, insofar as psychic pressure yields new realities.

There is folk belief that our thoughts or words create good or bad angels. Good or bad spirits. Spirit touches spirit. Be careful what you wish. We open to each other, infinite otherness keeps opening. We might not be able to help what we pour into another person, mixtures of good–bad spirits are par for the course. It is beyond our power to know what we are doing to each other here and now. The Bible insists on the importance of feedback, learning what we do from results, knowledge through outgrowth. But fertile actions contain mixed spirits.

Judge not that ye be not judged. Thou shalt know them by their fruits.

It is a kind of spiritual "body English", you keep trying. Good intentions are real too, especially if the road to hell is paved with them. How real is goodness? Levinas says it shines through the radiance of the face, infinite goodness, caring, an orienting attitude, soul point. Heart to heart, face to face.

The fact that there is pollution does not mean the beauty of a sunrise does not exist.

Conclusion

We have a treasure, the human psyche. It creates/discovers beatific moments. Whatever we call hallucination goes on, as does dreamwork, as does grappling with and avoiding problems. We grapple with and avoid each other. We seek infinite hells. Hell by definition *is* infinite. We live in many infinites.

It is difficult to simply appreciate a limited something—a grain of sand, a seashell—infinity soaks it. Try to keep infinity out—it is quite an effort. Catastrophic heavens. Look at a tree and just see a tree. Tell that to Cézanne, Van Gogh. The tree is soaked with treeness and devours us. We paint it to keep it still an instant, so that its movement is released. Through the tree we paint aliveness, special ways aliveness lives.

Shall one be a murderer or write about murder? Is writing a kind of murder? We discover we are murderers, although it takes thousands of years to sink in. Murderous impulses run deep, basic rage. Rage—an early orgasm?

Control, brakes—not enough.

Alternate infinities qualifying, enriching each other, tasting face–heart connections, hearing–feeling resonance of voices: a path worth trying.

CHAPTER TWO

Psychopathy in everyday life

In 2006, I was driven to write a book called *Age of Psychopathy* (2006a), which I put online. Since that time I published the two main chapters in journals (2007, 2008) available on Psychoanalytic Electronic Publishing. I did this in response to what I felt was the urgency and consequence of political decisions of the moment, including the decision to go to war in Iraq. Now, over ten years later, I have had opportunity to think more about the nature and occurrence of psychopathy and would like to share some of my thoughts and observations. I claim no originality in what I write, just expression of felt concern.

It strikes me that psychopathy is one of many currents in human life, competing and fusing with other tendencies. Henry Elkin (1972) lists, among them, schizoid, collective, autistic, and communal tendencies. One might add hysterical, phobic, obsessive, and a good deal more. Psychopathic tendencies are often characterized by schizoid and compulsive elements.

In *Age of Psychopathy* (2006a), I emphasized psychopathic manipulation of psychotic anxieties. For example, leaders of our country gave threatening warnings that Iraq had weapons of mass destruction. Political leaders evoked annihilation dread in the service of presumed self-interest, survival, and power. The cost of actual human life in this all too real fantasy script was sacrificed to egocentric–nationalistic redress of injury for 9/11, although Iraq was not a main player in the latter. A kind of displaced revenge on a country that was not responsible for the wound we were avenging. Perhaps Iraq provided an easier, more consolidated target to organize military operations and propaganda around, whereas the actual enemy, a terrorist organization, was dispersed, difficult to find and contain. Some, too, suggest that Middle East oil and the desire to be a strong force in that region played a role in hitting a weak, strategic target. An affirmation of partly imaginary self-interest via accusations and vilification of a relatively easy target, at least perceived so.

It may be that what we call psychopathy is one part of survival drives, for example, need for food and a relative modicum of safety. To kill is part of life. Even vegetarians destroy living plants for survival. I am touched by the beauty of ancient cave paintings, a kind of ritual celebration of the hunt. An association of the sacred with murder seems an ancient experiential element. Nations and smaller groups draw on it today, inspiring individuals to sacrifice themselves for country or other valued causes. To die for one's country, group, or cause is revered and celebrated. People die on many altars in the service of ideologies created by others.

Psychologies of influence have been with us a long time. We used Mesmer's name to tag a sense of one mind controlling another. Freud was fascinated by hypnotism, which played a role in delineating states like idealization, identification, transference in individuals and groups. Socrates pointed out the role of "opinion" over knowledge in the life of states and minds. Terms like "mob", "crowd", "collective", "mass hysteria" touch this tendency. It has been described throughout literature. A play I saw in college, put on by fellow students, Arthur Miller's *The Crucible*, indelibly brought home the role emotional contagion plays in life and the power of those who can shape it.

Group and individual psychopathy often go together and reinforce each other. We tend not to see dropping atom bombs in Hiroshima and Nagasaki as psychopathic. It shortened the war and saved American lives, a strategic godsend.

But it is hard to avoid seeing a surplus bravado element in such show of power, a number one gorilla beating its chest in triumph, subjecting an aspiring foe to abject submission.

Sometimes, seeing deformed will to power at work in deranged ways in lone outliers can heighten our sense of a thread of human nature too easy to justify under threat of war. Espy (2015) describes ways a serial pedophile and murderer insinuates his way into victims, entering them as a kind of "nematocyst that adroitly threads a barb into the body of its prey to inject their toxin and paralyze its victim."

In *Toxic Nourishment* (1999) I trace processes in which the child or baby takes in emotional toxins fused with nourishment. This seems a far cry from the willful channeling and use of toxins to mesmerize and control single individuals or groups, but suggests such capacities are there to be used if one can tap them. The popularity of films about mad scientists attempting to control the world is one instance of how people vibrate to psychic underpinnings. Tausk (1933), a fascinating figure in psychoanalysis who committed suicide, wrote about an "influencing machine", a diabolical machine operated by an enemy group controlling the victim, expressing a sense of one mind controlling another at a distance with evil intent (Eigen, 2004a).

Espy (2015) notes that the serial killer, David Brown, changed his name to Nathan Bar Jonah, a made up Biblical name (Nathan, son of Jonah) emphasizing his godly link. Bar Jonah wrote in jail, "I am the force, the me that lives inside you."

It is not necessary to explicitly identify oneself with God, but it is hard to avoid noticing that such a link is often made in murderous activity. One feels justified by a greater power. People who murder in the name of ISIS justify their actions as godly. Similarly, Al-Qaeda believed they were enacting a higher morality. We often assert U.S. power in God's name. Both Germany and Japan felt aligned with a superior cause in the Second World War. A god-sense in human life mobilizes great force.

Freud linked infantile narcissism with majesty and god, His Majesty the Baby, His Majesty the Ego. Caretakers cater to the baby, although baby also can be subject to abuse. Whatever one calls it and however one couches it, the "god-force" plays a strong role in psyche and society. Nathan Bar Jonah, victim of abuse, abuses others, sensing a power, a force, entering and taking the other over. Bion laconically notes links between god–dog, omnipotence–impotence, power–humiliation. The Bible says do not murder, but many murders are done by god-struck individuals in revenge for sin or maltreatment, to right a wrong, including national and international mass murders. For two of the greatest mass killers, Stalin and Mao Tse Tung, the "god force" was a political cause, transformation of society for the greater good.

Lone individual psychopaths often die on the altar of their deranged godly ego, giving their life and lives of others to assuage and rise above wounds that threaten to bring them down. One asserts a kind of godly right over life and death, perverse *quasi*-transcendence, above all, over all, worship of the "me" with the right to do as one wishes. Wishes that are gripped by compulsion to cheat, injure, or destroy, enslaved by a tyrannical will that drives them. Some few might even eat their victims, showing an archaic survival need, eating others to sustain life and support one's own existence. Language expresses such inclinations with images like "maw" to depict how life eats life and we eat each other and our very own self. At this level, shame, guilt, disgust play minimal roles because we are simply trying to stay alive, even when we eat ourselves up alive. Surely, if mother can say, "You're good enough to eat," one may feel like treating oneself to a nibble of one's own personality as well. Perhaps we are trying to make the shame, guilt, and disgust go away, make the bad feeling go away, make the pain of life go away.

We use claims of survival to justify a lot of bad things, although Freud points out the urge to destroy works both ways, turning against the other and oneself, double-edged, a momentous formulation with many applications.

* * *

Many currents meld in human life in varied keys. We do not call an animal psychopathic when killing another animal for food. Or even when an animal seems to take pleasure in asserting power for its own sake, the fun of maiming or killing without eating. One might call this a form of practice, contributing to survival, but there could also be a surplus of pride and enthusiasm that is part of pleasure. I have seen one animal taunt another in a show of dominance. If, in human life, these tendencies go haywire, in extreme cases we might get a serial killer who thrives on subjugation and lust for humiliation. We can call such actions monstrous but we can see them in play throughout nature. Survival makes its own laws. We know the repeated justification: I did it to survive. Psychopathy is, in certain ways, a branch of survival tendencies.

We are affiliative beings with many modes of attachment. Ancients wrote of many forms of love, self-sacrifice, and care. At the same time, they bore witness to uncaring self-assertion at the expense of others, murder and torture in service of power and pleasure. In our highly cultivated world, we speak of financial "killings," an area of predation that has come to the fore, gaining increasing attention in some quarters, overlooked, ignored, or even praised in others. One might speak of "financial abuse" along with other kinds of abuse, including sexual, emotional, mental in family, politics, and many kinds of groups.

As mentioned earlier, killing is part of life. Some would argue that war is normal. It has been asserted that many, if not all, nations are formed by force. Venice resisted dominance by Rome. It valued its independence and succumbed by force to become part of what became a unified Italy. The revolutionary and civil wars were essential for unifying the United States, not to mention the force that went into annexing Mexican territory and land occupied by Native Americans, and much more. One can trace histories of force between groups and what are now countries to earliest beginnings. We see groups in various phases of hostilities and consolidation, for example, in the Middle East or Africa, where tribal and religious identities compete for territory and dominance, poorly modulated by central influences. In various ways, we see this happening in our own front yard. Less than a century ago, Europe was subject to horrific struggles. I used to joke that "shalom" (peace) is a greeting in Israel because there is so little of it, a grim joke with wide application. The biblical priestly blessing includes as its nucleus a wish for peace in a life with so much war.

In *Kabbalah and Psychoanalysis* (2012), I write of a Rabbi Nachman story that touches an aspect of the human condition. He noted wars between nations, groups, within the family between husband and wife, between parents and children. He then asks, why is it people go mad when they go into the forest alone to meditate, and answers: without anyone to fight with, one fights with oneself. One needs someone to fight with. Surely, this is not *the* answer to the war within ripping ourselves to shreds. But it hints at one element, Freud's image of turning aggressions out-in, in-out. Freud died still wondering at the fate of destructive urges.

Fighting for survival, power, or dominance has been a subject in history and literature. Shakespeare paid a good deal of attention to war as drama and explored drives, ambitions, and vulnerability. He had a keen eye for psychopathic self-assertion as well as thwarted love. The Western canon of literature begins with an erotic theft that provokes war and travel (Eigen, 2002). Power can work by being sly, sneaky, hidden as well as a show of strength. One can feign weakness and even death to gain advantage.

When viewed against spectrums of survival mechanisms, psychopathy can seem pretty normal. In many ways we are prone to participate in the psychopathy of everyday life. It is hard to survive the day without at least some measure of psychopathic behavior. Philosophy, literature, and common sense have long debated the place of selfishness–altruism. Imaginary and actual situations are cited to support briefs for and against each tendency. Part of Freud's account suggests ways we move or fail to move from a self-centered to other centered orientation or, at least, acknowledgement of the existence of others and their claims for goodness. There are psychologies that proclaim basic badness or goodness or both, and try to account for one by failures or gratifications of the other. We are at sea, at once acting as if we know more than we do, while throwing up our hands in frustration and despair. Poets like Rumi support making room for contributions of all our tendencies. Each has come in handy at some point in history and each can contribute to the richness and growth of the whole. How to do that is question and quest. There are problems without obvious solutions and threads that explore unknowing as a generative state are also part of the mix.

We have many opposing tendencies. Freud's writing is a catalogue of binaries and spectrums of states and tendencies that work with and against each other. Sadism–masochism, exhibitionism–voyeurism, aggression against the other–aggression against the self, loving–hating, egocentric–allocentric, towards–away, fusion–opposition, the list continues. Tendencies and states can be over- and underplayed, magnified–minified. For example, we can feel too much and/or too little fear, shame, guilt, excitement, disgust, desire. We can experience hyper–hypo combinations of myriad qualities and intensities of states and tendencies. One moment, we deflect aggression outward to avoid turning it inward. Another moment, the reverse. And, more subtly, both at once in varying degrees.

Elkin (1972) writes of ineffable self–other states involving terror, agony, rage, bliss, and time–space organizations that might be called, autistic, schizoid, paranoid, hysteric, psychopathic, collective, communal. He tends to see our task as use of capacities with a primacy of the personal–communal, a lifelong process.

Psychopathic tendencies can become cut off from balancing capacities and wreak havoc. Any capacity or sets of capacities can be cut off from others. There is much emphasis in spiritual and political history on how to integrate parts–wholes. In aspects of mystical Judaism, there are writings about putting God's name back together, as though God has a tendency to break apart and we are to unite the YH- with the -VH. Breaking apart and coming together runs through world and personality and wherever we find ourselves there are unifications to make. One can imagine possibilities of nullification–unification throughout the cosmos, culture, and personality. A way Freud encapsulated this involved ongoing interplay of unity–entropy, life and death drives. Each tendency has a role to play in growth. Building up and tearing down are parts of creative work (Eigen, 2004a).

* * *

How do tendencies to hurt another become relatively divorced from concern? One factor might be a sense of having been injured justifying a wish to injure, a situation that can begin in infancy yet happen anytime. If you attack me, I might feel justified in attacking you. It might also be that I carry a sense of injury from early in life that diminishes concern about hurting others.

This can apply to groups and nations as well as individuals. If you invade my country and attack my cities, I feel justified to kill you in self-defense. While many soldiers are traumatized by battle, some report being released, freed from guilt over aggression. The freedom to aggress can prove a problem back in civilian life. One has to train oneself to hold back, not jump the gun and over-react to everyday situations as if they contained a danger requiring quick or harsh action.

Elkin (1972) writes of moments when an infant feels no concern about hurting mother because she also hurts him. Winnicott (1982) speaks of an infant's ruthless, pitiless needs, demands, and attacks. He conjured up a moment in which an infant feels as if it destroys the mother, the world, existence, but is assured of the other's realness by the fact that the other survives. The fact that the other survives the infant's destructive urges and fantasies makes otherness and life outside the infant more real. When the infant puts together that the mother it hates is also the one it loves, concern for the other in face of one's urges begins to grow.

Another combination of factors appears in Winnicott's observations about delinquency. He felt that juvenile delinquents may have enjoyed satisfaction that they lost. They try to steal pleasure that was stolen from them. They try to fill the loss by whatever means they can. Ethics or good behavior becomes less important than replacing the lost object, state, pleasure, or good by actions they imagine will do the trick. Elkin adds a sense that if no one gives me anything, if I am going to have something in life I must get it myself, an attitude that justifies getting away with things as long as I get what I want or think I want. A notion that plays a widespread role in a version of "independence" and "self-reliance." I picture Paul Bunyan jumping out of the womb and cutting trees, jumping over necessary phases of dependence with all its wounds and pleasures. To some degree, you might say psychopathy is a defense against deprivation as well as growing from it. In our economic world, never-enough couples with increasing indulgence in place of real scarcity and abundance.

I have heard a story about the village thief who was caught and brought to the Zen master. The latter advised putting him in a halter and carefully raising him on a tree limb. Then, while he dangled, bring him everything he wants. The story is a parable about being in a dependent state and being given to, touching a need to experience dependency and receive. Psychopathy is partly a denial of dependency, which nevertheless comes out in taking from others.

War is made of complex dynamics that illustrate tendencies at work in daily life in less explicitly violent ways, although there are many outbreaks and in-breaks. We tend to speak of love of country and need for sacrifice. Idealization of our side, demonization of the other. Sacrifice suggests sacred. War as sacred duty. I grew up during the Second World War. There was a sense that we were doing holy work, on the side of God, God on our side. Not just a practical, realistic matter, a dirty job that had to be done—Hitler had to be defeated. There was mythic surplus that inspired self-giving. We bathed in the Good, a holy bath of blood.

Idealization and death often go together. Idealization is often part of destructive urges, even if the latter sometimes explode the former. A crazy kind of love supporting the need to kill for the sake of survival, a surplus of self-righteousness that overflows to situations less important for survival *per se*, for example, economic dominance, power, getting or maintaining the (Imaginary? Real?) upper hand. A mechanism bordering, if not reaching, psychopathic.

I said crazy kind of love, yet a lioness displays a kind of murderous love, admiring, licking her victim. In *Damaged Bonds* (2001b), I depict a kind of murderous love in tenacious parent–child bonds and not many weeks go by without reading in the newspaper accounts of love turning into murder. Bond is a word dense with meanings. *Deutschland über alles*. Over all. Thou shalt have no other gods before thee. Bion (1987) takes pains to point out the illusory (delusional?) notion of being No. 1.

One might see psychopathy as supreme realism. Or a person scarred by life, imprisoned by Numero Uno, oneself as the ultimate one and only. I once asked my Abnormal Psychology teacher, Professor Howard Hunt, about a difference between schizophrenia and psychopathy. He responded by saying the schizophrenic is open wound, the psychopath all scar tissue. Professor Hunt introduced us to Cleckley's (1941) *The Mask of Sanity*, a work on psychopathy that has been in and out of style and still has its champions. The phrase, mask of sanity, has applications beyond clinical psychopathy and can be related to Winnicott's depiction of a "false self" that displays some adaptive realism that can too readily fall into a destructive vortex. To somewhat rephrase Cleckley, psychopathic me first, me over you, can too easily move from destruction of others to destruction of self. Recall that Freud used the term death wish to mean my wish for you to die when you injure, cross, or outdo me. Later, he reframed it in terms of a death drive in which unities break apart, a kind of entropic movement of the psyche. A wish for my triumph at your expense and more, my wish not only for you to be defeated but die is a tendency that can split off from ameliorating tendencies and hypertrophy.

Another psychologist I admired, O. Hobart Mowrer, suffered recurrent breakdowns and, while in hospital, started "truth groups" modeled after medieval small village meetings in which everyone confessed their sins, public confession. He and others found these groups helpful, although his depressive tendency remained. He committed suicide at the age of seventy-five, a couple of years after his wife died.

He accomplished a lot of good in his life, partly through his work as President of the American Psychological Association. People afflicted with serious mental problems can do a lot of good, although we tend to hear more about those who inflict their pain on others.

In one talk that I heard, Dr. Mowrer was asked to say something about psychopathy and responded, "Some people don't have the common decency to go crazy."

I am reminded of a sign a CEO had on his desk, "Show No Pity." And a well-known politician who was asked how he felt when he lost an election replied, "I cut my nerve endings long ago or I couldn't do what I do."

Can you imagine people with cut nerve endings running countries? Or perhaps the cut is only partial, muting, downplaying, or eliminating guilt, shame, and some kinds of fear, so one can push ahead.

We know how disappointed, downtrodden, and humiliated Germany was after the First World War, partly owing to the way they were treated in defeat. There are many possible responses to pain, humiliation, loss. Hitler and Wittgenstein were in the same class in school. What different directions they took. Wittgenstein came from a financially advantaged, emotionally challenged family. Three of his five brothers killed themselves, failing to meet their father's attempt to turn them into captains of industry like he. Wittgenstein found another way. Later, he referred his sister to Freud, although his critique of Freud is complex. She did mental health work with imprisoned juveniles. As Merle Molofsky wrote in an email note, "Some traumatized people invade a school and slaughter children, others will become health care providers."

At the time I wrote this, many of us were caught up in the United States 2016 presidential election campaigns. When I think of the grandiosity of one of the candidates, I think of his brother's suicide, as if self-attack and grandiosity are counterparts, whether fused or opposed. No two families are identical, but the archetypal theme of brothers who make it or fail is ancient. Anything I say is imaginative elaboration as I cannot know the intimate truth of realities at hand. I can only speculate and construct. It is as if aspects of the psyche divide up like characters in a play and *vice versa,* grandiose fulfillment of the father's ambition for one brother, abject failure and rejection for another. Donald Trump's older brother did not seem cut out for a financial, real estate existence. He had another kind of temperament and did not climb the money ladder. Yet, he had a different attraction to heights—he loved to fly. As we know, he was abjectly rejected by the father, became alcoholic, and committed suicide. One wonders if Donald's seemingly grandiose self-assurance is partly a defense against suicide. I doubt things are so simple. We are made of many ingredients.

If such counterparts are active, then splits–fusions–oppositions–oscillations may occur not only between success and failure but also between ascension and destruction. A split-fusion between self-aggrandizement/victim can be seen in Trump's discourse, filled with self-inflation, deflating others. He portrays himself as strong, rivals as weak, describing himself in almost messianic terms and describing others as corrupt, degraded, incompetent, or unable. Terms that come to mind include identification with the aggressor, splitting, magical thinking, self-idealization, denial, projection, manic defense, utopian–dystopian delusional thinking, manipulative canny.

Most political campaigns in my lifetime have been marked by praise and disparagement but I have never felt this level of fear about a candidate by so many. I heard about a class of black children asking if they would be shipped to Africa if he were elected. Tony Schwartz, the ghost-writer for Trump's autobiography, called him a chronic liar. A number of people thought of the film *White Heat* with James Cagney, a successful narcissistic–psychopathic gangster who climbs to the top of a globe filled with oil, fleeing the police. His last words, the police firing at him, "Made it ma! Top of the world!" Then boom!!! Are people only imagining the destruction the wrecking ball side of Trump would bring? We read that, in a security briefing, Trump repeatedly asked why we cannot use nuclear weapons.

There is a lot of pain in the world and people say they are doing badly, unable to make higher wages to keep up. We are told part of Trump's appeal is that he "gets" the hurt of others and will do something about it. Does Trump "get it" or is he doing a version of what has been done for many years—getting people to vote against themselves and their own interests, playing on resentment, discontent, class, race, tuning in and manipulating. After all, he promises to lower taxes for the very wealthy while his opponent says she will raise them, a cornerstone issue that gets blurred by wishful needs and hopes.

We are misled by the media world we live in, a world of hype and pictures, news frenzies, hysterical feeds. We see the rich and famous and hear about their amazing wealth. It obscures the fact that life is much more difficult and always has been, and, as human beings are subject to themselves, always will be. Fantasy life obliterates real life and appreciation for real daily existence as it is.

For many, Trump began as a cartoon, an underside of Disney world. We hear that part of his success was at the expense of others. We are sobered by his talent for turning aspects of what he senses into soundbites that appeal to the wishes of many, if at times in hallucinatory ways. How real is his "reality show"? We have nothing to fear but fear itself becomes we have everything to fear if "I" am not elected and nothing to fear if "I" am. I am that I am. A kind of *manic I* invoking dire anxieties in service of manipulating others and possibly oneself. Yet, I am afraid to say he is a mild version of a "Trump spirit" in the world, infectious affective attitudes and forces he weakly represents and expresses.

The world has outlasted, and will outlast, all of us. It is still going after atom bomb blasts that should not have happened. There have been worse times in history, yet I am not sure I have ever lived through a crazier moment of abrasive fragility. Tension between self-hate and self-love increases. Some feel it intensely. In others it works invisibly or, as Freud suggested, through disguises, causing so much damage in so many. We are more than compliant–defiant beings. Can we, little by little, discover ways to offset self-hate with deeper love? Not the self-love of egomania, which tramples others and damages oneself as well. There is another love, deeper love, that helps, or tries to. We have a deep need—but I cannot quite say what it is. Faith is part of it, but it is much more.

* * *

If we fail to learn how to work with psychopathy we will fail to address our psychopathic society. There is a huge psychopathic streak in our society and economic world: psychopathy of everyday life. We once were bewildered by psychosis and borderline psychosis but have begun to grow capacities needed for the work. Response capacities for work with psychopathy need to grow. It is imperative that the human race address its psychopathic side, more so than ever.

It was taken for granted that psychoanalysis could not treat psychopathy. A certain modicum of devotion to truth was necessary for patient and analyst to work successfully. Psychopathic tendencies in Freud and Jung did not escape attention, yet both made enormous contributions. The dictum that psychoanalysis cannot treat a liar seems questionable, considering the ubiquity of lying and the fact that the psychoanalyst is also a liar. It is not null-sum. Psychopathic tendencies in the mental health field are rampant, yet many are helped. Lying and truth, fact and fiction, imagination and reality are mixed in human life. A lot depends on balance, quality, and tone of spirit.

Our minds grew up as survival minds. Hiding, tricking, aggression helped us live in dangerous environments. At some point, we developed concern not just for physical but psychical survival, who and what kind of being we are. Capacities to work with ourselves are still embryonic.

All capacities play a role along the way in different contexts in varied forms. Bion (1994) notes that even stealing can aid growth, as when grave robbers of Ur, braving the revenge of ghosts, penetrated the Queen's chambers 200 years after her burial. Bion felt a statue should be made in their honor, a thrust forward of ambition and scientific greed in face of superstition.

We have a mind that has grown up to win, to survive, to stay alive any way it can, dealing with issues of personal integrity and expression, a work very much in progress. Where will we go together? How does each of us navigate our mixed nature, contribute to growth of possibility, honor the wound of being human?

CHAPTER THREE

Image, fullness, void

Images have often been looked at as second-class citizens in Western thought. For Plato, they were useful to help climb the ladder towards Pure Idea. Sensation, image, feeling were potential facilitators on the way to Pure Form. For Aristotle, the goal was to reach and exercise the pinnacle of cognition, active reason, a divine attribute. In philosophical writings, one could hear sensation and images spoken of as dregs, less than real thought, at best a support to feed thinking and be transcended. Similarly, wisdom, understanding, and knowledge are near the top of the Kabbalah Tree of Life, although all functions play a role if properly sublimated, head purifying heart, working with what heart cannot handle. There are variations, but this line of value has been dominant, an exception being mystical experience.

This led to a "control model" of the psyche, wherein higher controls lower functions as a practical and rarefied goal. The control model has had some success and been productive up to a point, but failed to solve the problem of human destructiveness, which takes place from top down as well as bottom up (Eigen, 2004a,d, 2011, 2012, 2014a,b,c).

Little by little, sensation and image and feeling began to get their due, although they always were first-class citizens for poets (a reason

Plato was suspicious of poetry, although he was a philosophical poet himself). Image stood somewhere between sensation, feeling, thinking, fed by and feeding all of them. I once gave a course on image as a linking function between sensation and thought.

By the eighteenth century, a philosopher, David Hume, could say, "Reason is the whore of the senses" or, rather, "slave of the passions," which for him included the senses and images they gave rise to. Distrust of reason as well as the senses and images was in the air, as suggested by Martin Luther's earlier (sixteenth century) dictum, "Reason is passion's whore" or "bride". Still earlier, St Paul discovered that "the things I would do, I can't; the things I would not do, I do." Knowledge was not enough and, it appears, ignorance was not the only or main lack that needed remediation.

William Blake, who spans the eighteenth and nineteenth century, already was working themes of doubleness, which intensified in the nineteenth century with the Romantic movement and Freud (Eigen, 2004a). Image and feeling became gateways of knowledge. Blake called Jesus poetic imagination and the Devil pure energy (Eigen, 2001, 2004b).

Wordsworth's definition of poetry as "emotion recollected in tranquility" does not mention reason. Rather, he appeals, with many other writers of his day, to processes we might call reverie, or some form of free association, where one discovers and follows tracks of resonance. Freud, who was considered by many to be a rationalist and by others a romantic, was exercised by head–heart–genital relations, with variable emphases in different passages. If a rationalist, in his creative work he also advocated letting the horse (unconscious life) lead the rider.

In the twentieth century, *gestalt* psychology saw inherent organizational processes working at the level of sensation and perception without needing to appeal to higher functions in order to create order. There were, too, spontaneous processes of organizaton on physical levels that, in one form or another, carried through evolving dimensions of experience. The nutritional workings of our circulatory system or solar bodies organizing in relation to each other to make our solar system are examples of physical *gestalts* in process. *Gestalt* psychology especially emphasized perceptual organization, the way the world is given to us as a field of experience, aspects of which Merleau-Ponty (2013) made a basic part of his philosophy.

In the USA, Emerson emphasized a "creative power" and, in the last century, Susanne Langer (1941) developed a philosophy of symbolism and feeling. One senses kinship with Henri Bergson's (1911) work on creative intuition which, one or another way, is a thread that plays an important role in psychoanalysis today (Bion, 1970).

Lacan (2006; Eigen, 1981) tends to associate image with animal signals, signs of territory, mating, predator–prey, and the like. In early writings, image is part of a nexus of ego control and seduction, having to do with an image of being more whole than one really feels and foisting this imaginary double off as reality, part of a desire to capture the other's desire. Desire is a complex term in Lacan's or anyone's work. With a little turn we can partly associate the desire to look good or seem more whole than one really is with Kohut's (1971) writings: imaginary wholeness as a defense against fragmentation.

My own penchant, along with many colleagues, is to emphasize the contribution of all tendencies, states, functions of personality. A bit like Rumi welcoming all inner visitors in "The Guest House" (see below, p. 14). In a related fashion, Blake described heaven as war between all voices of the personality benefiting all. Jung placed great emphasis on "active imagination" and Husserl on "free variation in imagination", the former to open contact with the depths and the latter use of intuition to discover structures of experience.

The above are a few of many touchstones, parts of larger currents in which experience seems to be finding new ways to value itself, tired of one side putting another down. It might be that our being is beginning to tire of dominance–submission or predator–prey relations and is seeking–creating further dimensions of living. As many have said, we are possibly just beginning to learn how to relate to and use the amazing psycho–physical–spiritual–social capacities we have. Bion (1990, 1994) felt psychic life was embryonic. Nicholai Berdyaev (1975) called it "neonic", related to neonatal.

We find many spectrums of experiential possibilities vying for recognition, sometimes working well, and often not knowing what to do with each other. We are growing accustomed to a task of lifelong learning how to be with oneself and others, what we are made of, what is creating us and how to partner our complex, mysterious makeup. As I grow older, ways of relating appear that I had no idea or sense of before. Buddha's advice not to string the instrument too tight or loose is barely a beginning. Jung made an inroad into potential psychic democracy by calling attention to how people organize themselves more or less around sensation, feeling, thinking, and intuition. Winnicott (1992), a strong spokesperson for psychic democracy (he thought there was very little of it), tried to support a wide range of psychic capacities. In the following passage, he lends support to functions often regarded as inferior:

> Some babies specialise in thinking, and reach out for words; others specialise in auditory, visual, or other sensuous experience, and in memories and creative imagination of a hallucinatory kind, and these latter may not reach out for words. There is no question of the one being normal and the other abnormal. Misunderstandings may occur in debate through the fact that one person talking belongs to the thinking and verbalising kind, while another belongs to the kind that hallucinates in the visual and auditory field instead of expressing the self in words. Somehow the word people tend to claim sanity, and those who see visions do not know how to defend their positions when accused of insanity. Logical argument really belongs to the verbalisers. Feeling or a feeling of certainty or truth or "real" belong to the others. (1992, p. 155)

Here, Winnicott emphasizes image, although it is with words that he makes his case. He notes a widespread attitude of better–worse, superiority–inferiority, rather than mutual enrichment. Herbert Read (1965) felt that image preceded idea by about two hundred years. We see explicit appreciation for many kinds of experience growing over time, including worlds that image mediates and opens, adding color and expressiveness. In *Lust* (2006b), I write of sensation as ineffable and see its fulfillment in poetic imagery.

Bion (1994; Eigen, 2011) associates image with creation, memory, and digestion of experience, a part of what he calls alpha function, the ability to store and use creative life. He does not reduce alpha function to image but notes the importance of image in mediating alpha function. There is much in Bion that goes beyond image, dimensions that for him are not representable at all. A tension between image and no-representation takes us to the edge of what can be communicated.

When we read that we are created in the image of God, yet God has no image and is not subject to representation, what are we to think? Where shall we look? As I take my daily run in the park and pass others or others pass me, I see so many faces and backsides—

what shines from them is God's image? Or is the image invisible within, ineffable. Is there such a thing as invisible images? I suspect so. Right now we are accessing this line of thought perception with words, word images. But I also feel much that words cannot convey. Wordless, imageless experience.

The *Lankavatara Sutra* (Suzuki, 1932) speaks of transformational processes going on in "Buddha lands", beyond representational access. The Wurzburg school of psychology in the nineteenth century found "impalpable awareness" to be part of problem solving (Eigen, 2011). Einstein (Ghiselin, 1952) wrote that he thought in images and vague muscular feels, which he later translated mathematically. He also remarked that he thought only once in his life—I wonder where that leaves the rest of us?

The null dimension has been with us at least since the invention of 0 (zero), and experientially probably long before. I can imagine the *satori* of individuals who hit on this notation, at last giving expression to a state that was with us forever, background achieving foreground. The word image of a world created from nothing, or void, hints that states of nothingness, void, emptiness, chaos (another domain) remain as part of the background of personality. Rabbi Schneerson (1998) spoke of God creating the world from nothing every moment and Marion Milner (1987) wrote Bion's O (notation for unknown emotional reality in sessions or unknown ultimate reality in general) as 0 (zero). I would personalize Rabbi Schneerson's statement. In a profound sense, you and I, our very beings, are being created, re-created from nothing moment to moment. How can this be so? This takes us to a mystical dimension in human life that has been a thread of human history before antiquity.

Mystical experience has run a spectrum of possibilities, with emptiness–fullness two extremes. Milner, attracted by Eastern spiritual writings, wrote of "pregnant emptiness". Both empty cup and cup runneth over are *bona fide* aspects of mystical states with correlates in everyday life (Eigen, 1998). Bion (1970, 1994) links emptiness–fullness with the baby at the breast, referring not just to milk but emotion. Minimum–maximum emotion. Now we are feeling more filled, now more empty. This can apply to a waxing–waning of the life feeling, now more or less alive or dead (Eigen, 2004c). All of this is part of expressive language creating and transmitting verbal images of inner states and tendencies. This can happen with images of sound as well as sight, as when Keats describes a Grecian urn with word images and hears "spirit ditties of no tone." Buddhism may emphasize emptiness and Catholic mystics fullness of union with God, each giving expression to richness of human capacity, *sunyata* and *pleroma*.

A man I worked with, Harris, moved in session from image to sound to imageless–soundless grief and joy, to some extent expressed through words, a kind of verbal imageless-image. It began, as one of Bion's (1994) examples did, with a church spire coming out of the rich abyss of childhood, Sundays in church with his parents, which confused and enriched him. He at once felt stultified and free. His spirit resonated with a feeling he had no name for, perhaps a sense of the holy or reverence, devotion, mystery. A mystery that daily life drained but Sunday church focused, at least for moments, living between stultification and spirit.

"I think it was a dream . . . church spire. I see myself in church with my parents. Images of saints and the holy family in semi-darkness, candles. I couldn't say what I felt but I suspect something like awe. Like going to the theater but with an extra halo. As a child, I lacked language for spirit. Spirit meant ghosts or was fused with ghostly fright. The Holy Ghost was frightening and it took many years to begin appreciating the Presence of the Holy Spirit in my daily life. As a child images of ghosts haunted me, nebulous presences that could tickle my feet at night if they accidentally fell outside the covers. They filled my closet. I dared not open it till day began. I tried with all my might not to think they were under my bed.

"I liked kneeling down in front of sculptures of the saints. I felt they helped me. The very fact that they were not alive and that I did not know them made their help seem more possible. Now I think it was because help from parents and others was so mixed with hurt. The world, the real world outside caused pain. People were painful.

"I had stomach aches, headaches, earaches, pains in my legs at night and nightmares woke me shaking and sweating. Yet, oddly, compared with day-pain, night-pain was almost a comfort. It didn't really occur to me that body, soul, mind had their own pains. The pains that came from outside were the ones that counted most. I looked forward to going to sleep, getting under the covers, and being away from outer reality. There was much in waking life I liked but the relief of night, with all its dreads, was a reprieve.

"As I'm talking I think I see a spire superseded by a steeple, still the church of my childhood. It is morphing as we speak into churches I've gone to as an adult here in the city. Gen appears, a young woman I loved who died from cancer before she was forty, kneeling in a church she went to downtown. She had wanted to be a nun. I loved being with her. She made me feel good for no reason at all. When she touched me, I laughed. She would say, 'Why are you laughing?' I felt she knew but she looked bewildered. I thought she was feigning. 'You know,' I'd say.

"Finally, one day the truth came out and when she asked why I was laughing the words came, "Because you delight me." She tickled me with delight. It must have taken over half a year for that to happen. Where were the words hiding before? I really didn't know where and then they were there. A free moment, a bell ringing. 'Can you hear it?' I asked. 'Hear what?' she asked. 'The bell ringing.' 'No,' she caught on, 'but I can feel our ringing hearts.' "

As I heard this, I thought of a bell I saw in a glass case in Ireland. It was supposed to have had a pure, perfect tone but now was cracked. I thought of a meditation gong I was given as a gift when I spoke in Seoul. On holidays, I ring it as a signal for guests to begin sitting at the dinner table. I tell the children to come close and when the sound dies out I hold it close to their ears and they can hear the soundless sound continue. They are mesmerized, in pleasure, awe. The sound runs through them and you can see it in their faces. I think of the pure sound of the Irish bell and the soundless ripples of the Korean meditation gong akin to the soundless sound of the universe by which all sound and music are tuned, a bell of no tone that sets all tones. A tuning fork for the music of the spheres, music of the soul. Harris is crying.

"I'm with Gen in the hospice. She has faded into coma yet still is alive for me. She looks like she is sleeping. I feel if I kissed her she would kiss back, her eyes would open. I touch her hand, kiss her cheek and imagine she stirs. She was so open-hearted, the most open-hearted person I knew."

We said no more awhile. Harris sobbed. I felt with him. I thought his tears were part of what the universe was made of, what I was made of. Then he looked at me with one of the most sincere looks I ever saw. Little by little I began to see a glow.

"Such joy," Harris quietly says. "I never knew such joy existed."

"I don't think it's something you ever lose," I said.
"No," he said.

He seemed relaxed, just sitting. Images and phrases began running through my mind. "A thing of beauty is a joy forever" (Keats, *Endymion*); "A light is lit for the holy" (*Kol Nidre*, Arnold Schoenberg, Opus 39); "A flame of God is the soul of man" (Proverbs); "Light for me a light and I will guard your light" (Yom Kippur service). I thought of the Jewish custom of lighting a twenty-four hour candle each year on the date of a close one's death. Partly a remembrance, but also to help raise the soul of the departed to a higher and higher level. I was feeling Harris helped raise my soul; through him, Gen lifted us both.

I told him about the Jewish custom of a memorial light and he thanked me and said he was going to light a candle that very night.

I suspect it goes without saying that candle and flame has been an image of spirit as far as we can remember. There is much in our world and being that dovetails, conjoining inner–outer realities.

The session moved between words and wordlessness, sound–soundlessness, image–imageless. Word image, visual image, and sound image meld.

Readers of my work may know part of the significance the story of Job has for me (2011, 2013). I tend to see the Job story as a mystical journey. The loss of everything in his life is a movement of contraction. Everything is taken or cut away until nothing is left but Job's contact with God. Plotinus asks, how does one find God, and answers, "Cut away everything." At that point, God shows off his power, asking Job, "Did you create and play with Leviathan, the earth, the sky, sea and all there is?" Job is given a panorama of the miracle of existence, image after image, brought to silence in face of God's presence, a point of contact, essence to essence. At that point Job bursts out, "Now I see You in my flesh." Not only does Job see and feel God, his whole body does, flesh, cells, pores as well. The remainder of the story charts a movement of expansion, new family, honor, work. All that has been taken away returns in a new key and more. The mystical vision and encounter creates authentic faith not known before. "Now I know You in my flesh."

Contraction–expansion, heartbeat, breath, circulation, pulsation of organs, muscles, nerves, feeling. A basic rhythm of existence, one I call a rhythm of faith (Eigen, 2004d). In Job's case, contraction to an alone point where only God exists, then expansion of a new sense, divine abundance in all existence. From wealth to poverty to the greatest wealth of all, mediated by Grace of Divine Presence.

Movements of contraction–expansion or, for that matter, attraction–repulsion, taking in–pushing away, work at physical and emotional levels, one mirroring the other. The terms themselves are verbal images of felt events in which different dimensions of existence feed and image each other.

Job, in a deep sense, provides a set of narrative images for Plotinus's depiction of one kind of relationship to God, from the alone to the alone. The *Zohar*, a central text in mystical Judaism, includes another set of images, marriage of the soul with God's feminine presence, the Shechina. Divine wedding between man and God and between masculine–feminine aspects of God, a visionary sense of new wholeness. Wedding as a linking image between broken, fragmented, dissociated parts of existence. Inner marriage of man with anima and woman with animus is an important part Jung's imagery. There are many variations one can work with. A person I see speaks of his wedding with the Divine Mother. Women I have seen also have expressed a complex link with the Divine Mother, union and opposition. Many threads to pull.

Jung also wrote his own version of the Job story. As he neared the end of his life, both the Job story and inner marriage seemed to grow in importance, the latter playing a central role in the wake of a heart attack.

After the heart attack, Jung (1989) drifted in and out of dream-like states and had a strong sense that the Kabbalistic wedding was taking place in him. He experienced being wed with Shechina, God's feminine presence, an intense, personal consummation of the *coniunctio* archetype. He published a number of images depicting aspects of the divine wedding within. A wedding not only between humanity and its soul but all Israel and Divinity and also male and female parts of God, repair of primordial breakage.

Jung's images of the wedding showed significant knowledge of the *Zohar* and mystical Tree of Life. He was well aware that a climactic moment in the *Zohar* was the wedding of one of its main heroes, Rabbi Shimon bar Yochai with the Shechina, and, in his dream-like state, Jung felt that *he* was Rabbi Shimon and that it was *his* wedding. He was profoundly lifted by the divine wedding within. Somewhere in

Memories, Dreams, Reflections (1989) Jung writes, "I was the marriage. And my beatitude was that of a blissful wedding."

In the *Zohar*, Rabbi Shimon announces on his death day that he is not married, although one of his sons sat near him as he spoke. It was not his enduring earthly marriage that he spoke of, but the divine marriage that was to come at the moment of death, a moment that came with the Shechina's kiss, divine union. So much in Jung pivots around uniting opposites and in Kabbalah the divine union is beyond all opposites (Eigen, 2014c). Story, image, feeling fuse. Suffused with wonder.

Rumi's poem, "The Guest House", mentioned earlier, is a poem about welcoming all parts of personality as one would honor guests. Each day many feelings arrive. Joy, sorrow, cruelty, shame. Welcome them all, says Rumi. There is much to learn from each. All of them may be guides from beyond. A momentary awareness can open worlds, making space for experience you could not have imagined. You can find Rumi's poem online (here is one version: www.gratefulness.org/poetry/guest_house.htm). It reads like a guide for therapists, something steer by.

It is a little like the Jewish tradition that you never know when you might meet Elijah. A stranger you bump into, a beggar on the street, a head of state, people at work, your love (love–hate) at home. Any encounter might open worlds. The tradition says more—any encounter might save the world.

Rumi goes farther, setting the scene within your being. The stranger is you, your feeling world, affective attitudes, how you organize experience and are organized by it. Rumi is very close to Bion when the latter says the therapist's job is to help introduce the patient to himself/herself. Rumi's emphasis is on self-introduction, introducing yourself to what you can experience. In related fashion, Bion's dictum about introducing the patient to her/himself, goes for the therapist and therapy too. Each session may teach a therapist more about what therapy is and can be and further introduce the therapist to the work of intuition.

Do not give up on yourself, although giving up also can open realities. There are many Zen stories of the seeker failing to achieve enlightenment and finally letting it go. One failed seeker decides to simply tend his garden. At least he can create something beautiful, a delight to eyes, scent, soul. At least he can avoid doing too much harm. Then one day, least expecting it, he stubs his foot on a rock and—it happens. The breakthrough, the opening.

Elijah is close at hand, nearer to you than you are.

In earlier work, I have noted three dimensions of experience (there are infinities): (1) just plain me; (2) constant struggle; (3) Grace. Of course, they intertwine like samsara–nirvana or hell–purgatory–heaven. One teacher I worked with, an old Chassidic man, once told me he does not believe there is a hell. When we die our soul goes to the cleaner, is cleaned up and readied for heaven. There are endless combinations and possibilities. All these stories are made of images and images filled with stories organized by affective attitudes (Eigen, 1992). Affective attitudes act as frames of reference for experience and dream figures express them.

I have often written about becoming partners with our capacities and evolving together. The kind of model Rumi proposes, his own version of partnering ourselves, has not been dominant in history. Nonetheless, many voices express it and it keeps on taking new forms. Perhaps it has its own growth trajectory that we are in some way contributing to. It is an alternative way of approaching the human psyche and our experiential life, very different from control and domination, a different self-image, image of being and personality, very much in progress.

CHAPTER FOUR

Where are we going?

We are born all life long and, as psychoanalytic students, part of this process involves ongoing psychoanalytic births. Graduating from a psychoanalytic institute is like being born from a psychoanalytic womb, an extended, intermittent process of birth. Curious to liken an institute to a womb when entering it might be a kind of birth, too. What a strange new world one enters, for some a sense of home. I remember the first one-on-one session I had with a patient when I began training. I felt I could breathe in an emotional atmosphere I had been looking for without knowing it. A new kind of atmosphere to live in, mind to mind, heart to heart, soul to soul, psyche to psyche, with all the quagmires, blocks, furies, longings, and beauty therapy gives birth to. Therapy wombs filled with therapy births and persistent conflict whether to be born or not, in what ways, with what price. It can be confusing to be in and out of womb at the same time, but to be so, I feel, is a basic structure of our existence.

There are ways every birth involves a partial death. In experiential life, births and deaths are partial and interweave in myriad ways. Therapy hopes to support a balance for the better, on the side of gestation, expression, and what Winnicott depicts as basic creativeness in the sense of being alive.

William Blake writes of a moment in each day that Satan cannot find, which, if rightly placed, renovates every moment of the day. Special moments, creative moments which he likens to pulsations. I would not go so far as to say we find such moments in therapy, but we do find something like them, creative moments, creative sessions, sometimes more, sometimes less. It is the creativity in therapy, special forms of creativity, which cements the deal for many of us. To be a therapist almost guarantees a creative life.

As time goes on, for many, therapy creativity becomes both womb and birth in which all manner of creatures grow. A lot like a psychoanalytic institute, in which all kinds of things happen, hurtful, uplifting, enlivening, deadening. Very like a family, or neighborhood, or nation, therapy wars go on within and between kingdoms, along with inklings of the possible impossible and the impossible possible.

Lacan likens therapist and patient to lover and beloved who switch roles and affect. One could also experience therapist and patient as warriors, unsure if murder or cooperation is best. Sometimes, on reading Freud, I wonder if he is fantasizing gladiators, the unconscious as lion, thumbs up or down, mutual mutilation or partnership. The idea of partnering ourselves, each other, and our capacities seems almost a newcomer in evolution next to the model of control and dominance.

All kinds of things go on in psychoanalytic wombs. Tendencies, states, inclinations, sensibilities, capacities compete, fight, interweave, nourish. I think of Yeats's famous words, "what rough beast slouches towards Bethlehem to be born." I think, too, of experiences as a child lifting up rocks in the woods. Who knew what one would find, strange looking critters, crawly, wiggling things, menacing, enticing, scary, mesmerizing. Therapy narcissism or, as Sir Edward Dyer wrote in the 1500s, "My mind to me a kingdom is." Entranced with the psyche, one's inner being—what discoveries are on hand for psyche and us? What surprises?

When Bion spoke in New York City in 1977, the only analyst on these shores he referenced was Theodore Reik, his writing on surprise. I fear Bion modified it somewhat, saying, "Life is filled with surprises. Most of them bad." One reason the good feels so good. Like Reik, Bion emphasized the unknown as an essential part of experience, making for humility of approach and a call for compassion.

Given the complexity of what we face, I sometimes like to substitute "Love thyself" for "Know thyself," although the two can nourish each other. What a momentous job we have, to help support growth of capacity for psychic contact with an attitude of compassion rather than cruelty. Psychic cruelty—where does it lead us? We see its work so many ways, in and outside us, an evolutionary challenge.

Personally, I have learned from every psychoanalytic "school" I have ever come into contact with. Not just because of intellectual curiosity, but the inner need for discoveries each makes or emphasizes. Each adds to my sense of psychic reality and adds to what may be useful in a session. By an accident of life, more than sixty years ago I studied Jung before Freud and my relationship with each are still growing.

Many schools are part of my background. Gestalt psychology, body therapies, depth and humanistic psychologies are among those that found ways of nourishing each other. The list grows. So many groups that have so much to give fight each other. I would like to declare the therapy wars over. Is that unrealistic? We need strife to grow? Even so, some modicum of transcendence might be possible, making room to nourish what we can offer one another.

In my sessions with Bion, I was taken aback when, seemingly out of the blue, he said, "I use the Kabbalah as a framework for psychoanalysis." It opened and reinforced a sense that psychoanalysis needs something more than psychoanalysis in order for it to be psychoanalysis. It needs, of course, Life, but also a sense of the many approaches to living humans have explored. Perhaps someone might have a musical sense of psychoanalysis or an aesthetic sense that exceeds, yet embraces, psychoanalytic possibilities. Many models are part of Bion's writings, but with me he made sure to bring out the spiritual.

When I was young, I would sometimes think that the human race was made up of different species with little means of communicating with one another. Why do we have so many kinds of psychoanalytic schools and other therapies, so many kinds of spiritual disciplines? We might as well ask, why do we have so many different kinds of poets or musicians or artists or languages?

We seem to inhabit a variety of psychic territories with a variety of sensibilities. William James classifying people as tough or tender-minded had some vogue and is a verbal image still current today. Ancient Greece suggested four main temperaments. Jung, very like Kabbalah, notes individual emphasis on sensation, feeling, intellect, and intuition. One could suggest other schemas, but it has not escaped notice that people have varied traits which play roles in how they do or do not get along. If you fail to find a school or group that reflects your particular sensibility and makeup, you might start your own. In a way, fighting for causes is akin to fighting for the kind of person you are, or imagine you are, or perhaps would like to be.

We have a large cafeteria of psychic possibilities to work with, to partner with. Fighting at times is useful but can be overdone and become a barrier to larger perspectives that allow for differences, expected or unexpected, known or unknown. Differences even in oneself. Rimbaud, we know, said, "I am an other." Groddeck had a cosmic-like sense of the It. There is no end to the fathomless within. Both depth and surface are inexhaustible. When we look at another school, we might say, "Thank you for mining *that* part of personality *that* way." It is a kind of spontaneous division of labor. One group, one school, one individual, cannot do it all. *All* is not something that is ever done.

It was quite a struggle for art, dance, music, or poetry therapy to become part of psychoanalysis. But today they are, or can be, depending on the practitioner and those s/he works with. Today, many forms of body work and psychoanalysis interweave. Marion Milner was one of the early spokespersons for body and art in psychoanalysis. Winnicott, we know, used drawing as part of his work. Lines between child and adult therapy became more permeable.

Today, I would like to say, many venues can be part of psychoanalytic work. Cognitive, behavior, focusing, imaging, sensory are some of the modalities that can be incorporated. Psychoanalysis is spontaneously evolving in open ways. So much can be put to use that dogmatic closing-off of possibilities is out of place. Neurological research and thought has always been part of the background of our work and continues so today. We are all in this together, up against tough issues of the day. Mutual appreciation of contributions that can help will, one hopes, grow more widespread.

As I mentioned in the NPAP graduation talk I gave in 2010, Bion felt that psychoanalysis is embryonic. He also speaks of it as a baby with possibilities of development as yet unknown. He did not hesitate to speak about politics, music, poetry, science, philosophy. He noted that psychoanalysis grew from experiential vision through literature (e.g., Freud's reading of Sophocles' *Oedipus*), the importance of which Freud never denied.

Can I be silly? Picture Freud as Don Quixote. Remember, he learned Spanish so he could read Cervantes in the original. Picture psychoanalysis as a dream of Cervantes. In Bion's last, extended written work, a semi-psychic autobiography, *A Memoir of the Future*, he writes of psychoanalysis as a dream and the dream of psychoanalysis. There is no contradiction between such deep non-sense, sense of humor, and the spirit that psychoanalysis touches with its fairy wands.

Have you found, as I have, that many analysts consider their work sacred? One size does not fit all and I do not want to fit one person into another's sensibility. The other day, on leaving for work, I offhandedly said to my wife, "I'm heading for shul." My temple. My prayer, a special place of faith and challenge, psychoanalytic faith and challenge. To work within a state of prayer—have you ever done that? You do not have to, of course. No need to be any kind of analyst other than the one you are and will grow into. I am just saying a little of how it feels to me, at least sometimes.

It is a relief to leave one's ordinary life and enter this special altered space without LSD. Just the living psyche. Hide and seek, living and dead. The invisible phone rings, you pick it up and what does it say? "Hello, psyche speaking." And you dip in. And yes, it is true, when the swim ends and the whale spits you up, it feels good to leave and go home to ordinary living. Unless you discover, as many do, that ordinary living is extraordinary living. Sacred spaces grow. I think of Jacob running away from Esau, making an unexpected discovery on a hillside when he thought he was alone: "You were here and I didn't know." This special You that may be Everywhere.

And what about the sacred space of psychoanalytic writing, the writing cure? Would psychoanalysis have been born without the support and impetus of writing? Free association practiced first with writing, then spreading to the spoken word, speaking and writing egging each other on? I used to teach the Freud–Fliess letters as part of a course on creativity. What a treasure, still pregnant.

Bion felt that psychoanalytic writing should try to evoke the experience that gave rise to it, part of the emotional reality of the session. To touch another from the place that touches one—to touch and be touched.

Do you know people who write only to and for themselves? I know many. Such an important form of self-contact, what Balint called an area of one, an area of creativity, part of self-creation or discovery, a valuable part of what might be a widespread autistic dimension of being. Psychoanalysis as an autistic as well as dyadic or triadic activity—all important contributors. And yet, autistic contact with oneself is truly relational, a relationship to the feel of one's own being, and through oneself *being* itself. A contact that grows in depth and breadth all life long.

What is therapy all about? It can be about all kinds of things. One of them involves fanning a vital spark, an image used by both Winnicott and Bion. Kabbalah says there are sparks buried everywhere and our job is to bring them forth, let them work. No matter where we find ourselves, there are sparks to be found. Perhaps sparks within are created by the finding itself. Finding is part of creation.

Here is a little quote from Bion's Paris Seminar in 1978, the year before he died, the year after he was in New York:

> I come across a lot of what is thought to be scientific psychoanalysis, but it doesn't remind me of anything except boredom. The situation in the consulting room, the relationship between these two people, could be like the ashes of a fire. Is there any spark which could be blown into a flame?

He then wonders if a better word for the "consulting room" might be atelier, the artist's workroom, and asks the analysts present, "What sort of artist are you? Are you a potter? A painter? A musician? A writer? In my experience a great many analysts do not really know what sort of artists they are."

I would like to end here with a note on psychoanalytic beauty. But I cannot end without talking about some aspects of the world today. In 2006, I wrote an online book called *Age of Psychopathy* (2006a), largely in response to decisions made by the Bush administration. I felt one strong dynamic of the time was psychopathic manipulation of psychotic anxieties. I spoke some about this at the graduation talk I gave in 2010, but it seems even more germane and portentous now, heightened, among other things, by the 2017 presidential election.

Psychopathic manipulation of psychotic anxieties. For example, manipulation of annihilation threats to gain an upper hand, or get what one wants or thinks one wants, particularly in the realm of power.

It was taken for granted that psychoanalysis could not treat psychopaths. Earlier, it had been assumed by many that psychosis was also a lost cause. Yet, today, many of us successfully work with psychosis and a later offshoot, "borderlines." Care and capacity have stretched and continue to grow. Are we also making, can we make, inroads with psychopathy?

When I was younger, I heard over and over that you have to have a certain capacity for truth for psychoanalysis to work. Psychoanalysis was about truth. Psychopathic tendencies in Freud and Jung did not escape my attention, yet both made amazing contributions that continue to help this moment.

Psychopathic tendencies in the mental health field today are part of everyday life, including therapists and analysts. You cannot psychoanalyze a liar seemed like an odd conclusion, since a liar was doing the psychoanalyzing. As I grew, I realized the double- and triple-edged work of lying. Things are not so simple. Psychopathy of everyday life is very real.

By the time I reached Bion, I was ready for his declaration that "lying is ubiquitous." If you cannot psychoanalyze a liar, you cannot psychoanalyze anyone. Of course, there is quality and degree, different kinds of personality organizations. But I think we have already begun to take a bite out of this particular apple and are working in more complex ways in the face of human destructiveness. You who are graduating today are at the forefront of this evolution and will contribute in your own personal ways to growth of the capacity to navigate our mixed nature. One never recovers from being human and how to be and work with ourselves is a work in progress.

Now I feel a little freer to speak about one of my deepest feelings of all: the beauty of this work. Those who have a vocation to save the world through social and political reform have potential to help humanity in large ways. I learned about myself a long time ago: my calling was to try to help individuals one on one. Little changes can make a big difference in someone's life. Freud talked about small changes in quantity having a big effect on quality, a shift in the big battalions of life and death for the better. One helps, I feel, in a large way indeed, by adding to, lifting, one person's sense of existence.

I have spoken a lot about birth in this chapter, particularly therapy births. Throughout our lives we are pregnant with our lives, pregnant with unborn selves and psychic babies, including thoughts, feelings, attitudes, modes of experiencing. A pregnancy that never stops, no matter how many births. Gestation does not end. The real question is, can it begin, to what extent, with what quality?

There are so many birth murders in the world, in our lives. Think of all the violence in pockets of the world we are aware of, and all that we are not. So many murders sound like an odd form of self-affirmation, self-assertion. So many have a suicidal component. I remember the day when the saying, "I'll feed you full of lead," was current. Think about a murderous feed. The idea of committing suicide in the act of murder seems more total. There are different kinds of feeds and fusions of assertion–surrender. And now, what seems like a newish addition, taking a "selfie" and broadcasting it on the internet as one murders others and kills oneself. Perhaps murder and suicide have always been "selfies" in some ways.

There are so many currents of our being, all with contributions to make if a good enough affective attitude acts as a larger frame. A modicum of self-transcendence in ways that enable multiple currents breathing room, without turning things into a "stomping ground for wild asses."

For as much of my life as I can remember, I have been struck by Beauty. Keats: "A thing of beauty is a joy forever." In the most awful circumstances, a moment of beauty has saved me. In *A Memoir of the Future* (Bion, 1990), there is a scene of a man running from the enemy. Bullets are flying, escape seems unlikely, and he happens to hear a bird singing and looks up, and for a moment is lifted beyond his plight. Later, in relative safety, although not out of danger, he recounts it as one of his most beautiful moments, a heightened reminder of the good of existence he almost lost.

Beauty is the center of the Kabbalah Tree of Life, radiating in all directions, surfacing even in hell on earth. It reminds me of a Zen saying, "There are good days even in hell." And Congressman Rangell repeatedly telling people, "Every day is a good day."

In my book *Faith*, the chapter entitled "Can goodness survive life?" I write,

Beauty, I believe, is one source of ethics. To see something beautiful can arouse a sense of goodness. Not only a sense of feeling good, but also a sense of wanting to do right by, wanting to do justice to, a world which can be so beautiful, which can so touch one to the depths. (2014c, p. 1)

I will close with words of Bion, a moment of permission, again from one of his last seminars:

It is very important to be aware that you may never be satisfied with your analytic career if you feel that you are restricted to what is narrowly called a "scientific" approach. You will have to be able to have a chance of feeling that the interpretation you give is a beautiful one, or that you get a beautiful response from the patient. This aesthetic element of beauty makes a very difficult situation tolerable. It is so important to dare to think or feel whatever you do think or feel, never mind how unscientific it is.

As graduates, your job continues to grow as midwife of psychoanalysis as it midwifes you. May your births be blessings opening needed realities, known and unknown. In our different ways and walks of life, midwifing and undergoing birth processes is a central part of existence.

CHAPTER FIVE

Thinking about squirrels

You get to know a lot about animals when you trap them. On numerous occasions I have trapped squirrels in my roof and attic. The first time we had squirrels in our house I called an exterminator. He trapped and got rid of them and closed the holes they made. Within several months they were back. Since then, I have trapped them myself with better results. The time between occupancy has grown, sometimes years.

Why I should fare better than professional exterminators, I do not know. One guess is they let them go too near our neighborhood. I learned from experience they have to be let go very far away. Even across the Brooklyn Battery Tunnel connecting Brooklyn with Manhattan will not do. I do not know how they do it, but if you let them out just across the tunnel in Manhattan, they come back. I took to bringing them to Central Park uptown across from my office, where they seem to stay. That is some sixteen miles from our home in Brooklyn. Distance is crucial. Leaving them out in Prospect Park in Brooklyn less than two miles from our house will not do. They will be back within a day or two. They have a strong nesting attachment. I do not know if I would have learned that about squirrels without this experience. They so often are scampering about every which way looking for food and fun. Closing holes of entry is useless if they are determined. They are very strong and persistent.

A few weeks ago, after several years of not having them, they arrived and took up residence. I might even tolerate them but for my irritation at being woken up anywhere from 6–9 o'clock in the morning with their thumping and scrambling above. I try to turn over and shut them out, but sooner or later annoyance wins and I begin to plot what to do. In addition, past experience shows that if they are given free reign, they will start to eat some of the wooden beams and alarm wires, setting off the alarm and making it impossible to set. They can cause a lot of damage just by being themselves.

I decided the first thing would be to see where they were coming in and out. It did not take long to locate an opening under the roof drain, where they came and went at will. I borrowed a trap from my neighbor, who said I could have it for two weeks. They also were beset and would need it but did not have the time or ambition to do anything immediately. They were going to California to visit their new grandchild and hoped the squirrels would vanish in their absence. We both wished the squirrels would go away.

It is against the law to poison a squirrel as you can a rat. In any case, having dead squirrels in your walls is not an appetizing thought. Not being allowed to kill squirrels (they are so "cute") has some protective value for the house. We use a trap made by a company called "Have a Hart". You put a little peanut butter on a tray linked to a wire system that automatically triggers a door to slide shut when the tray is touched. You then take the caged squirrel far enough away before opening the closed door. The squirrel usually races away in a flash.

The noise was loud and persistent in the early morning and I decided to put a trap on an outside ledge near the opening under the roof drain. I secured the trap with rope under a shut window. There are some false starts getting the leverage right enough. The trap can shut too soon, too late, or not at all, so that sometimes squirrels get the peanut butter and leave and sometimes they get shut out. Eventually, through skill and luck, the trap shuts and locks the squirrel in. It is here my story really begins. Different squirrels show different reaction patterns upon discovering they are trapped.

Many begin by banging against the trap doors, chewing on the steel mesh with their teeth or scratching at it. If persistent, some of the metal mesh gets coated with blood. The first squirrel this trip banged against the doors, chewed and scratched the mesh and rested. It repeated this intermittently, and eventually the rest periods became longer. The banging, chewing, and scratching diminished and stopped. For long periods the squirrel crouched or lay quietly, as if waiting for the next thing to happen or giving in to the limitations of the situation. Eventually, I took the trap down, placed a garbage bag around it to minimize stimulation, and let it sit outside by our garage till my wife and I had a chance that evening to drive it over the Verrazano Bridge and release it in Staten Island by a wooded area. It raced out and disappeared so quickly I began to wonder whether it had been in it at all.

The next day a second squirrel was caught. This one did not stop banging against the cage or chewing at the mesh. It did not rest, at least not for long. It kept throwing itself against the barrier or chewing it. I had never seen a squirrel so relentless. Pavlov felt animals have a "freedom reflex" and this one reacted against enforced confinement with all its might without let-up. When I went a few hours later to take the cage out, the squirrel was near dead. It was the first and only one that died from this procedure in all the years of doing it.

The third squirrel trapped a day or two later behaved a little differently from the first two. Instead of trying hard to get out, it spent a long time eating and licking every trace of peanut butter possible, licking the plate clean. It managed to find out parts of the mesh that had some peanut butter on it too, inadvertently smeared by my fingers while setting the trap. It missed nothing and kept at this activity until it was satisfied that it had gone beyond diminishing returns. It made gestures to get out, some banging and running back and forth in the small space, and then laid its head on the metal plate where the bait had been and rested or seemingly slept. When night came, we took it to Red Hook, another part of Brooklyn and when the cage was opened, he began speeding in the direction we came from. My wife said, "It's going to beat us back." But so far we have not seen it.

The fourth and last squirrel alternated banging against the door, licking the bait plate, chewing the mesh and resting. It rested, too, on our drive to Queens, where we dropped it off by a fishing pier.

It appears that variations in patterns of response characterize different squirrels, sometimes a matter of life and death. We might fancy innate differences in temperament, sensibility, or ways of organizing experience. There was a pleasure-oriented squirrel who licked all hint of food, responding relatively mildly, compared with the squirrel who could not stop flinging itself against the confines of the cage until it died. Two others were variants in between.

If I let my imagination go, I picture individuals who have a hard time modifying a maladaptive response that might have benefits in some situations but not in others. Perhaps we are all trapped by innate–environmental organizations and hurl ourselves against the bars of our personality and being, trying to be free of the limitations of a particular life form. Are we stuck in a conundrum: if we became free of ourselves would we still have ourselves to be free from? Are we relative beings tortured by a need for absolute freedom? Perhaps we can become a little freer from ourselves than we now are and live with the un-freedom that seems a necessary part of existence. How many kill themselves, unable to bear the confines of their own being?

It seemed as if some squirrels almost sensed waiting was necessary, that they lacked the key to solve the problem they were up against. I would not discount the possibility that some had premonitions of the possibility of change, that the situation might change with time and further opportunity would present itself. I wonder if some sensed they were being taken somewhere by a higher power and would be let go, an experience inherent in formative biblical stories. Perhaps many creatures experience oscillations of compression–freedom that are part of breathing and other rhythms of inner–outer weather.

I think of the story of Bodhidharma bringing Chan Buddhism to China. After an apparent mis-meeting with an Emperor, he made his way to a mountain retreat where he meditated before a wall for nine years. I do not know how much the wall changed (walls do change in many ways), but Bodhidharma evolved in grace and capacity. We face many inner–outer walls and something in Bodhidharma's attitude may help us (Eigen, 2011). Wilfred Bion expressed an overlapping perspective in his work, *Attention and Interpretation* (1970). So much goes on in processes of attention. Bion spoke of an attitude of being without memory, expectation, desire, or understanding, a kind of radical openness in which evolution of personality and being can grow. Much can happen in, as well as out of, our cage.

I think of a Zen story about a fly trapped in a bottle. It tries to climb up the glass but each time it gets a little higher it slips down. After repeating this exercise many times, it rests at the bottom, looks out, and after a while says, "Nice bottle." You might say Kant said the same, sharing categories and limits of existence.

Beckett's *Happy Days* offers a parallel parable. The heroine (or anti-heroine), Winnie, is stuck in a sand or rock mound. The times I have seen the play it felt like being stuck in a rock, the top half of her body "free" to move while the bottom half remains unseen below the surface. She could speak and move her arms expressively as well as access her pocketbook (a little like Batman's utility belt). By the play's end only her head was above the surface and she still found ways to say, "So this is going to be a happy day after all—sort of."

Willie, her man and companion, sits on the other side of the mound, his back partly visible. They cannot see each other but have a bond and find ways of feeling each other's presence. Near the end of the play, Willie finds a way of moving towards Winnie's side of the mound and creeping up towards her. It is a failed connection in some way also real. One cannot avoid hearing the word "Win" when Willie tries to call her. A seemingly endless fount of "happiness" covers failure and wounds.

I could not help wondering whether even the wound was happy. A happy wound, happy unhappiness. Psychoanalysis might call this denial and manic defense but it reaches deeply into a wish for good. One wonders at the survival of tendrils and filaments of life in the unlived, almost invisible good in depths of desolation.

When Beckett's therapy with Bion was ending, Bion took Beckett to a talk by Jung. Jung was talking about a woman patient who felt unborn. Beckett leaned over to Bion and said, "That's me!" To be unborn all one's life is not so unusual. In various ways we remain embryonic. Nikolai Berdyaev spoke of "neonic" freedom, a neonatal dimension ever renewing, ever creating.

Beckett sought help, in part, because his attachment to his mother hampered finding his own life more fully. His two years with Bion played a role in increased mobility, moving to Paris and becoming the writer he needed to be. One can find themes in Beckett and Bion that echo each other but each had their own trajectory as well (Miller & Souter, 2013).

The image of being stuck in a mound touches a sense of not being fully born, half in and half out, an image with many applications. Birth goes on all life long, yet we remain born–unborn. I think of Kafka's sense that his life was an incomplete moment. There are ways notions of "complete", "total", "whole" can be persecutory. There are many pleasures in a semi-born life, even if one is partly stuck in stone.

It is hard for me to avoid associating Winnicott with Winnie and Shakespeare with Willie. Harold Bloom spoke of the importance of creativity for Freud. Freud said when he no longer could do any more productive work because of cancer pain, he wanted to end his life. And so he did a year after coming to England, 1939, on Yom Kippur. His letters to Fliess read like a creative journey. In a lecture I attended many years ago, Bloom linked Freud's love of creativity with God's creative love and the importance of biblical vicissitudes of creativity. After all, the Bible begins with depictions of God's creative acts and subsequent consequences. Freud felt creativity made his life worth living or, at least, was an important part of what sustained him. Bloom associated the birth of the human with Shakespeare, or, at least, a certain kind of human being, with increasing emphasis on subjective conflict. Freud elaborated this theme in his own key, opening further doors, even ways of being human.

Why do I impishly link Winnie with Winnicott? Winnicott's problems with sexual impotence were well known among his colleagues, who celebrated occasions when his analyst might say, "Winnie got it up last night." Winnie was an informal nickname for Dr. Donald Woods Winnicott in his milieu. Such "collegial" talk was in the air during the time of Beckett's analysis with Bion. Winnicott and Bion shared important common influences, although each independently went their own way. Bion wrote about the importance of sex and family for him. He had three children; Winnicott was unable to have children but was a pediatrician and child analyst. Both were extremely creative as psychoanalytic investigators and artists. Creativity, as with Freud and Beckett, was the center of their lives. As for "Willie", poet-dramatist, background presence, and Muse, I was struck at a young age by Shakespeare dying shortly after he stopped writing, left London, and returned to rural Stratford-on-Avon where he was born. My young mind could not avoid wondering about the conjunction of creativity and life.

* * *

I earned my psychology doctorate at the age of thirty-eight. A year earlier, my first two journal papers came out. Much that I learned in graduate school played in the background of my mind. For example, gestalt writing on problem solving. In one experiment, Sultan, a chimpanzee, was challenged to reach a banana suspended from the top of his cage. Inside the cage were a table, sticks that could be joined, and a chair. Sultan tried various ways to get the banana in vain. Standing on something, jumping, stretching, and waving sticks was not enough. Exhausted, frustrated, despairing, at a loss, Sultan sat in a corner, apparently depressed. None of his readily available responses worked. After some time, life came back, his face lit, he put the sticks together, placed a chair on the table and reached the banana. Kohler understood this as insight linked with reorganization of perception (Kohler, 1976). Sultan's giving up and non-action after exhausting his usual repertoire apparently helped create space for spontaneous regrouping of the perceptual field.

Pascal's depiction of mathematical creation includes pretty much the same phases. Working hard at a problem, giving up after exhausting all possibilities one thinks of and tries, then letting it go, giving time and space for incubation or relief (Ghiselin, 1952). Pascal tends to see what happens as development of intuition, the latter an important dimension for Bion. Sometimes, British physicists referred to the hiatus as the three s's: shit, shower, shave—moments that allow something to break through and dawn. Freud also describes letting go of conscious control and letting the horse lead. He used generic mythic–perceptual images, such as dark–light to depict creative processes (Eigen, 2004a).

So many dimensions interplay. Animal studies show the importance of environmental contribution as well as innate endowment and learning. In one study, rats were placed in environments that were too easy, too hard, and challenging enough. Rats are naturally curious, exploratory animals. Getting familiar with where they are aids survival. When the environment was too easy, physiological arousal levels were low. When too hard, arousal levels were high and paralyzing. In both cases, the animals became more sedentary, a bit like Sultan when he gave up trying. When the environment was challenging but not defeatist, the rats displayed optimal arousal level, interest, and exploration. When I was an undergraduate, my Ancient Philosophy teacher began the course by talking about the environment in ancient Greece: not so easy that little effort was required, not so hard as to be crushing, but hard enough to bring out growth of capacities.

Rats do not like to be in water, but if thrown into it they swim and make an effort to get out. If efforts fail, they float restfully until the situation changes and getting out becomes possible. Experimenters wondered what would happen if the stop trying response for some of the rats were surgically put out of play. The brain area that seemed associated with stopping was altered for half the rats. When thrown in water with no escape, the normal rats tried to get out and ceased futile efforts and floated as before. The altered rats kept trying in spite of lack of success. They persisted for a much longer time before the floating response began.

I wondered about the squirrel that could not give up or rest or regroup. Was it programmed to persist in face of impossibility? A biological variation, disposition, a need to persevere no matter what? The other squirrels tried more varied responses and eventually rested. Did they have more hope that freedom would appear or did they give up and give in, reconciled to confinement for the time? And we humans, what resources do we have in face of confinement, especially inner cages, confinements of our own beings?

In one case, limits can stimulate creativity: creative limits. In another, limits can feel destructive and inhibit play of what is possible. A child tells his father he did not want to play with other children in the park because it was boring. The father asks, "Was it boring or was it fun but you gave up?" The father senses something in his son giving up, sealing off engagement. Something he knew in himself that he worked on. Difficulty can evoke bits of wisdom as well as self-injury as part of self-preservation.

A woman told her friend, "I felt nothing. I feel nothing." She was talking about men she dated but women friends as well. Her life was dwindling to nothing. Only nothing was real. Everything else was pretend, superficial, not quite right or it. Nothing was meaningful. On the one hand, she felt this was awful despair. On the other, she felt it could mean a new beginning. She was being forced to recreate her life into something she could live. Destructive nothingness: the end of everything. Creative nothingness: seeking to build life anew. Who was doing this? Her makeup, personality, culture of her time? For the moment, what and why seemed less pressing than an urge to be born without knowing how.

To what extent can we let our life in? It is as if life has a need to be born in our feelings. Aliveness spans spectrums of possibilities, as does stillbirth and combinations we are. One Hollywood portrayal I happened to see involved parts of *The Eddy Duchin Story*, a semi-fictionalized film of the pianist–bandleader's life. I want to share moments of the fictionalized portrayal of the bandleader's relationship to his young son, Peter, who also became a pianist–bandleader. Peter's mother died five days after he was born and Eddy became an absent father. Nevertheless, son and father had deep feeling for each other in the film, and likely in real life as well. Here, fiction touches deep truth as well as falsifies it.

Eddy tries to get through to Peter, who will not hear that his father is dying. The son turns away, cannot listen, says things like, "You have always been strong, in control, there to lead the way." He could not bear to hear of his father's mortal weakness. "There is Something Bigger that controls all of us," says the father. The son turns away, withdraws in great tension, but something is cracking, thawing. "Do you understand me? Do you understand what I'm saying," the father insists, determined to go past the barrier. Finally, Peter says, "I think so." The feeling is palpable.

In a final or near final scene, Eddy and Peter are playing piano together, two pianos facing each other. You feel the joy, potentially tragic joy. The father's face conveys a sense of profound acceptance and affirmation of life in face of death. A kind of joyous relief that he and his son have let each other in, let the news, the reality, in. They are playing a grand, romantic piece together, something like Rachmaninoff, but I don't know. Both were playing well, fully, until the father's finger abruptly stops as it hits a key and you hear him fall to the ground. The camera stays on Peter's face as he continues to play and you sense he has let it in, let life in.

* * *

I shall close with some questions raised by the "case" of Daniel Paul Schreber (1842–1911), who wrote one of the most discussed first person accounts of psychosis, diagnosed by Freud as paranoid schizophrenia. I have written about Schreber and some of his cultural–individual formations in detail (2004a). Here, I touch only a few threads related to confinement–freedom, particularly self-confinement.

The book he wrote on his "nervous illness" was intended, partly, as a legal argument showing why a man like himself ought not be confined against his will. He hoped it would help get him out of asylum care and, indeed, he was released from his second round of confinements about the time his book came out, 1902–1903. He continued functioning until his mother's death in 1907, when he was again confined, this time until his death in 1911. Between confinements, from twenty-five on, most of the time he functioned as a respected judge. He was born in Leipzig and lived his life in Germany.

There are contrary interpretations of origins of his illness and its meanings. Here, I would like to emphasize personality's tensions with itself, whatever its roots. Schreber could be quite normal, carrying on intelligent, coherent conversation, so much so that he became a welcome dinner guest of the head of an asylum he was in. On the other hand, there were times when he became too overwhelmed with alternate states to function as usual. Nevertheless, in his second confinement, he argued there was no need for him to be kept in asylum against his will, that he was no harm to himself or others, and that his stream of experiences and ideas called delusional by medicine did not cause injury. I do not have a clear picture of the state that kept him confined after his mother died in 1907 for the last four years of his life.

His vocabulary is a kind of psycho-spiritual feast, replete with terms and functions linked with mystical experience and neurological research. Soul murder, blackout, a basic language, Divine rays, messiah, salvation, miracled-up souls and presences, spiritual voluptuousness, to name a handful. Whereas Aristotle conceived God in terms of what he considered the highest human function, active reason, Schreber's link with God was through nerve contact.

Neurology was in the air. Brain diagrams in Freud's gymnasium textbooks had commonalities with today's picture as well: for example, old brain–new brain functions emphasizing emotion–cognition. For Schreber, neurological images and ideas became lived experience. He felt himself turning into a woman in perpetual intercourse with God, not only through imaginary genital contact but real, lived nerve-to-nerve contact. Through continuing this contact, he was healing soul murder and saving the human race. One can imagine him saving humanity from a basic soul murder that runs through existence.

Schreber depicted a crisis with no resolution. Nerves mediated Divine rays and the experience of spiritual voluptuousness. If his feminine nerve contact with God would cease for an instant, the world would come to an end. Not simply his individual delusional existence, but all humanity and planet Earth. He was saving all of us.

Schreber also wrote of another ending, before his belief system was fully formed. The world as he knew it ended and came back to life in the spiritual form he describes in his book. The catastrophic end of everything already happened, then life was reborn in a new key. Freud spoke of a catastrophic loss of the object (other), the link returning in a hallucinatory way. Loss and restoration. Schreber called the end of the world a blackout. Then returning in a miracled-up delusory mode. One might say a caesura gave birth to psychosis or was part of that birth.

If one pulls out the emotional nuclei in Schreber's journey, we find common life themes. There are spectrums of loss–restoration, qualities and kinds of rebirth. We use terms derived from nature, like night–day or darkness–light to describe emotional experience. We are bound together by catastrophic anxiety, which Bion says links personality together, as does a very deep, precious sense of goodness. Schreber fought hard to preserve goodness as a thread in life. When we say life hangs by a thread, it might be good surviving destruction.

There are many complexities in Schreber's system we cannot take up here. Some I address in *The Psychotic Core* and there is a wide body of work on Schreber readily available, not least of which is his own documentation of creative struggle. But I wish to mention his "fleeting improvised men" that were souls transiently living in bodies by Divine miracle. On the one hand, life has solid structures. On the other, much valued experience is fleetingly improvised. So many living moments without name or image, but one senses them. So many felt presences. This reminds me of those angels God creates for given moments. Miracled-up enrichment. Or transformational processes depicted in aspects of Buddhism that go on without image, thought, language, and which all Buddhas who ever lived or will live aid (Eigen, 2011).

Schreber enjoyed spiritual voluptuousness, a kind of ecstasy with God. Yet, he and God were locked in constant struggle. All existence depended on this struggle. Should Schreber fail and lose God's grip, all would end. This was not just mystical surrender, but battle for control. Sadomasochistic control and surrender at the same time. In *The Psychotic Core*, I associate Schreber's focus on becoming female foreshadowing growth of cultural movements supporting female agency. In Schreber's vision, the whole world depended on the work of female agency for its survival. One hears an echo of links with

God's Shechinah, feminine presence and transformation schools emphasizing contact with other sides of being. Nevertheless, Schreber engaged in a life and death struggle, a complex situation that continues in many ways, involving work with multiple tendencies in personality, society, culture, politics. As Freud said about psychoanalysis near the end of his life, "The struggle is not yet over."

* * *

I shall end this chapter with a note on birth. We already mentioned Beckett's emphasis on failed birth. We are born all life long, a birth process that remains incomplete. If Kafka felt his life was an incomplete moment, we can add an incomplete birth.

Birth anxiety is an old theme. In one or another way, it is with us all our lives. There are many ways to be born and fail to be born. Death anxiety is part of birth. Life–death anxieties reverse, oppose, and fuse in countless ways.

Winnicott (1992; Eigen, 2004a) writes of trauma hitting as personality begins to form. A result can be that beginnings are marked by anxiety, whether creative and/or destructive. Fear of beginnings can lend a semi-paralysis to aspects of one's life or lead to injurious rashness. Anxiety is part of creativity but so is search, thrill, discovery. The phrase "in the beginning" is biblical but is also part of Melanie Klein's and D. W. Winnicott's discourse. Emphasis on "new beginnings" finds its way into many kinds of transformation literature. Winnicott felt a sense of creativity as part of living, inherent in being as well as doing. Yet, there can also exist not only birth anxiety, but also a force against birth, a destructive force attacking life possibilities. We have thought of many "reasons" for this force and ways it works, but the difficulties it presents remain unresolved. Thinking of Schreber's psychosis, one might say one survives or is born the best one can under the impact of one's existence.

CHAPTER SIX

O, orgasm, and beyond

O is a notation Bion uses for unknown, ultimate reality, in psychoanalysis emotional reality. One is tempted to play with "O" until it bites one: One, Oh, Omega, Open, Orgasm, Origins. Add your favorite O-words. Marion Milner (1987) called O 0 (zero), partly after Zen's *sunyata*, pregnant emptiness (zero is one of the evocative expressions Bion calls O).

On pp. 323 and 325 of *Cogitations* (1994) are what I call two O-grams. At the bottom of the tree with its branches, under the root, is O giving birth to all the tributaries of culture and psyche. For example, on p. 323, O gives rise to Root which gives rise to Instrument, God, Stone, Language, and Paint, which give rise to Music, Religion, Sculpture, Poetry, Painting. You get the idea: One giving rise to Multiplicity, the latter O-expressions.

The Sh'ma Yisroel has a similar structure: Sh'ma Yisroel, Adoshem Elokenu, Adoshem Echad. Hear, Israel: God is God the Many, God is One. Adoshem is singular, Elokenu Plural, both names of the One God (Eigen, 2012). It is an ancient image with variations in spiritual traditions and philosophy. The Big Bang in science has, in some sense, a related structure. Eddington thought the term "explosion" had no parallel in the ancient world but is packed with mischievous possibilities in science. Multiplicity proliferates from a singular Explosion. *The Zohar* also has an image of a dark spot exploding into the universe (Matt, 1998). Bion (1970; Eigen, 1998) relates Big Bang or an originary explosion to the beginning of the psyche and of consciousness, an explosion into being. Birth and development of psyche has an orgasmic element. He relates it, also, to psychosis, Big Bang an image of Catastrophic Origins in which flotsam and jetsam of thought, feeling, sensation fly off at accelerating velocity into infinite void, so that psychic products do not cohere, or cannot be felt, or are felt too intensely.

I have found many people in which both tendencies operate at once, or oscillate, as if there is a switch that turns feeling off and on. Now nullity, now hyper-intensity. An individual described feeling detached while immersed in satisfying sexual intercourse. He could have amazing orgasms yet be disturbed by a part of his consciousness witnessing the event, a blank onlooker or, as Bion (1970) describes, maximum–minimum intensity or emotion simultaneously or successively. My patient tried many approaches to what he felt as pain at the height of pleasure, which finally eased as he came to make room for both capacities (Eigen, 2002, 2006b). Wordsworth described poetry as "emotion recollected in tranquility," but for some both capacities operate together, heightened reflection and immersion at the same time. One person felt convinced he watched himself "go under" in infancy, a sense of seeing himself emotionally drown that never left him (Eigen, 2006b).

Existential literature speaks of self-transcendence as part of experience. As we experience we are aware of ourselves experiencing. In a way, we are in and out of it at the same time. Some make a negative judgment about this self-consciousness, as if it should not be there. Yet, it is part and parcel of being a human being. We are made up of multiple capacities that can confuse us. It is not a matter of doing away with any so much as learning to work together, an evolutionary task of becoming partners with our capacities.

We speak of dual aspects of experience, for example, detachment–attachment. Some spiritual exercises emphasize one, some the other. Quality and use of both tendencies are at stake. In *The Psychoanalytic Mystic* (1998), I write of detachment and attachment mystics with arrays of intellectual, emotional, and erotic dimensions. Wars have been fought over the primacy of one or the other: which is truer, more real. But they all play a role in the color of experience, adding to the feel of life. I sometimes wonder if wars between parts of personality and wars between groups of people will diminish together. William Blake (Eigen, 2001a) suspected it was a matter of ecstasy of difference, picturing heaven as war in which all voices of personality have maximum say to the maximum benefit of all.

Elkin (1972) uses the term communion (co-union) to describe aspects of co-unitive experience. That I very much appreciate moments of union indicates I am there to appreciate it. It is not simply loss of self or consciousness or awareness, although such a feeling may be part of it. It is, too, a union of distinct beings in which both poles are affirmed and enhanced: co-union, communion. There are many ways of being distinct and many ways of being in union, some more life giving or destructive than others.

I have called this double capacity two-in-one, one-in-two, a distinction–union structure, in which both tendencies are part of a structure that is made up of both dimensions, a paradoxical monism, a kind of psychic DNA/RNA (Eigen, 1998, 2011). They can be more dissociated or fused and take myriad forms in spectrums of experience. Sometimes we feel the forms they take are inexhaustible and sometimes we feel trapped in rigid organizations.

Kumar Shahani, an Indian film director, planned to make a documentary of Bion's life, to be filmed in India, where Bion spent his first eight years. Bion never got there; he died on the way in 1979. Shahani decided to make a film based on autobiographical parts of Bion's writings, especially *A Memoir of the Future*. He and Meg Harris Williams wrote the script. The shoots were in 1983 and never finished, owing to a combination of financial difficulties and human tragedy. The fragments (I almost wrote figments) shot can be seen online at: https://www.youtube.com/watch?v=MKVS7hhqUL4&feature=youtu.be. For some introductory orientation, click on Show More under the picture.

There are many ways to view the shoots: one is as an extended agonic orgasm. Like Bion's Big Bang, bits of thoughts, feelings, interactions, sensations afloat in expanding–contracting psychic space, earthly, hellish, purgatorial, and, in some ways, heavenly infinities. You might be surprised by what goes on in heaven. Sex, like all experience, is not made up of one thing; many currents go into it. Big O—a bit like white light—contains so many possibilities, a pleroma birthing all kinds of little o's, including all the demons in this world and beyond. Take any part of the film, any character or moment and ask, What part of what kind of orgasm is this? What kind of affect/sensation/thought/void state? Can you feel it? Reflect on it? Relish, cherish it, and move on? Stymied, still, antagonized, repulsed, and move on? Meltzer (2008) speaks of sex as labor, surely one element, but there is also Grace. We work the fields that sustain us and, as Saint Paul discovered, are taken to we know not where.

There are many kinds of orgasms: thought orgasms, feeling orgasms, sensation orgasms, psychic orgasms of countless hues. Orgasms that fizz out or are unreachable, that explode, tear us apart, ring bells of inexpressible sweetness and joy. Orgasms that are localized and circumscribed, orgasms that spread, permeate beyond location, through everything. And what is the Platonic Orgasm of Orgasms, the Ideal Form that all sensuous orgasms participate in and image, as when we say Adam, earth sentience, is made in the Image of God. It is, after all, a human being who uses the word divine to describe feeling that spreads through one's body and lifts existence.

Repeating the words "Who are you? Who are you?" is a Hindu exercise but it has avatars in other spiritual paths. One moment who are you is tormenting, irritating, numbing, another ecstatic. I remember a lecture by Hannah Arendt in which she spoke about the secret ecstasy of thought and intellectual work (Eigen, 2001a). How can one break through the wall to get to who one is, through the who are you to the thing itself, past the shadows on the cave wall, break the dark glass (Saint Paul: intimations "through a glass darkly"). An urge to get to the real real thing. Would that be an Orgasm of orgasms or something we have no name for? I always took Job's climactic moment, seeing the wonder and awe of God's reality, as a kind of archetypal mystical orgasm, as when Job says, "Now I know you in my flesh." Or perhaps we have gone beyond anything the word orgasm can encompass, to O itself.

I have had woman patients who complained that they reach orgasm too easily, not just through sexual organs, but by being touched anywhere. While it is a capacity to enjoy, it causes problems in the traffic of daily life, the workplace, when another frame of mind is needed. To be overwhelmed by porousness at any moment—a delight but also liability, depending when, where. One might ask, why is our world so limited that it has little space for orgasm anywhere anytime? I have known people who get off on reading stock prices, ups and downs, openings, possibilities—but I never heard that the Eros of money and numbers stopped one from figuring out what trades to make.

The unpublished script for the Bion film has more scenes than were made and, as might be expected, changes in the actual making of a scene, which involves spontaneity. In one scene that was not shot, Kathleen, the pregnant young serving woman in the film, is beseeched by her mistress, Mrs. Rhodes, in a role reversal, to reveal who she is. There are various role reversals in *A Memoir of the Future*, where the last becomes first. In the film, Bion's Ayah, who took care of him when he was a child, ends up on a throne, with Einstein kissing her hand and Man (who is also Satan and Saint Peter) kissing her foot. Kathleen in the film is a servant. In the unpublished 1983 script, she is also Mrs. Rhodes' daughter and a mother and something with no name, like God or Great Goddess, a secret creator.

Mrs. Rhodes is not satisfied by Kathleen answering, "I am your maid." She keeps asking, "Who are you? Show me truly who you are." Kathleen demurs, feeling Mrs. Rhodes could not take knowing, perhaps akin to Peter denying knowing Jesus. Knowing who she is is costly—one does not remain the same. Knowing who she is requires risk. Mrs. Rhodes persists and Kathleen begins to reveal: "I sent you artists, but you did not see; I sent you prophets but you would not listen . . . I sent you Bach . . . I sent you poets . . ." Mrs. Rhodes cannot settle for intermediaries. She wants the thing itself, the reality of identity itself: "But I want to know who you are."

Kathleen tries once more: "I am the Feeling that became Fact, the Fact that became Fiction, the Science that became Art, the Germ that became Phenomene. The cycle of rebirth is seeded in my womb. I have borne Athene, Goddess of Wisdom. I have borne the Great Cat Ra. I am a figment of your imagination. I am you, if you will become me."

A climactic moment has been reached, a moment of transformation, of becoming. A movement of becoming at the core of personality, an invitation to further realization. It is the necessary form of dramatic narrative that no climax is final, there will be more, just as no dream or thought or feeling is final. Life continues, more transformation is possible, even or especially in the most secret places, new intimacies. The psyche never stops. An orgasm that never ends, ebbs and flows, stops and starts, rises and falls, a never-ending secret in plain view.

There are moments in the film that can be seen as a kind of negative orgasm, orgasmic destructiveness (Eigen, 2001a). One such is mirrored by Heaton Rhodes (Kathleen's brother), a nineteen-year-old soldier in uniform like the nineteen-year-old Bion. He speaks of another soldier whose guts are blown out by artillery orgasms while Heaton roars with orgasmic laughter. Life heightened by destructive intensity. A kind of horrific caricature of birth, a deformity of the human condition marked by war.

Kathleen is pregnant throughout the film. In one scene that was shot, Fred Bion, Wilfred's father proposes to her and, against Mrs. Rhodes advice, she goes off with him. Earlier in the film, Mr. Bion made a pass at the Ayah, who easily evaded him. Mr. Bion and the Ayah were the help team that midwifed Wilfred's birth. If there was an orgasmic current, there was also a sense or fear that something could go wrong. Orgasmic life tinged with disaster, catastrophe as well as *jouissance*, a link, often painful *jouissance*. Off Kathleen goes, her arm in Freud's. In the film, this took place in heaven, an aspect of human imagination that creates or informs emotional fact, psychic reality.

For me, a meaning of Kathleen's eternal pregnancy has to do with our earthly challenge: will we, can we, give birth to ourselves and in what ways? We are pregnant with ourselves and in the course of life there are many abortions, stillbirths, miscarriages, and birth of many kinds of experiences, experiences of all shapes and sizes and colors. Pregnancy never stops, nor does the possibility of birth of experience (Eigen, 2014a).

Near the beginning of *The Zohar* it is written, "A rose is a rose and a Rose is a Rose!" (Matt, 2004). The special rose-feeling is usually taken to mean God's feeling for Israel. The rose reference comes from the mystical flower in the Song of Solomon, which the Saint James Bible translated as "rose of Sharon", taking its usual vivid poetic license. There is scholarly dispute as to just what this flower was and one neutral voice suggested simply calling it "a budding bulb!" Adin Steinsaltz (2006), a prolific mystic and scholar, writes of a "thirteen petalled rose". One might say a rose by any other name is still a rose—and if it is not a rose it is a Rose, a mystical flower that many names may express and no name exhaust.

It is a flower within—orgasmic sometimes, calm and serene other times. It may take many forms and volumes, but those who experience it tend to intersect at some point. For many years, one form it took for me, especially as a young man, was a heart vagina, a vaginal heart. There was a moment, while doing a bio-energetic exercise with Stanley Keleman, that my heart became a vagina, a feeling that spread and never left, deepening, evolving over the years (Eigen, 2014c).

A mystical flower is not unknown in various spiritual traditions. At times, a kind of inner orgasm, an opening of the depths, profound union and more than union, beyond union. A kind of soul invagination, vaginal hearts everywhere.

A patient, groping to share something he felt, confided a moment of opening after exercise.

> ". . . A quiet, vibrating feeling through my body. I was taken by surprise. Never quite felt this before. It was not the rise and drop of orgasm and needing to wait half an hour to try again. It was more like pulse tingling all through. Maybe women have orgasms like that. I've heard women speak of an orgasm spreading all through. They don't seem to have to wait long but can come one after another. I can't compare because I don't know. What I was feeling was not multiple orgasms. I felt a continuity head to toe, a soft petalled bell ringing through my body a tiny bit faster than my heartbeat. All I wanted to do was lie there and keep feeling. It makes me think there is life beyond orgasm, better than orgasm."

How many dimensions dance on the head of a pin? A physical body, science body, emotional body, mystical body. The mystery of feeling and feeling feeling (Eigen, 2004d, 2006a). Mystery is expressed so many ways. The mystical rose becomes the lilies of the field, which Jesus says to consider how they clothe themselves so beautifully through intrinsic growth. Chuang Tzu (1964) confesses there is so much creativeness that there must be a creative Master of this world he never saw, yet feels has identity but no form. Does feeling have form? Not visible, touchable form like physical objects. One feels feelings but not with the touch of one's fingers.

Freud (1900a) called consciousness "a sense organ for the perception of psychical qualities." Worlds of psychical qualities. No matter how we explain consciousness, something unexplained remains. The phenomenological circle: Consciousness is the medium of access to its explanations of itself. Consciousness sees and hears but cannot be seen or heard. More broadly, Eddington's (1929) remark about the universe: "Something unknown is doing we don't know what."

Bion's O as unknown reality links with aspects of Kabbalah (Eigen, 2012, 2014a,b). Here are some quotes from *Faith* (2014c):

> For Bion, faith is a vehicle that radically opens experiencing and plays a role in building tolerance for experience. At the same time he does not minimize what we are up against, the full force of destructiveness. (p. 58)

> As mentioned earlier, Bion uses "O" as a notion for "the fundamental reality". In Judaism, YHVH connotes a fundamental reality for which there is no language, concept, or sign. We keep reaching for what cannot be thought or imagined or said, but a term such as God, YHVH already seems so limiting. A formation already in a process of becoming a belief system, rather than the non-formable, open faith linked to what cannot be known. Bion called the latter "infinity", reminiscent of Kabbalah's *Ein Sof*, infinity, no bounds, an attempt to get beyond names like "God". We keep trying to find ways to touch, express, evoke the untouchable. "Infinity" also seems limiting. What is the wordless sense poets seek to evoke with words, or the imageless "feel" artists seek to evoke with image, or the Buddhists express with "emptiness". Perhaps these are ways we try to give expression to boundless, limitless moments, infinity moments, when walls fade. (p. 60)

> I often say about Rilke that he creates realities as he writes. His words create existence. Bion is terrific for this. Immerse yourself in a phrase, a section, a paragraph and speak, and reality opens, you open, some class members open. We are taken to places we did not expect and might not have reached ourselves. (p. 59)

Unknown to unknown. O as opening.

For me, in childhood, the Great Mystery of Opening would come unexpectedly, ineffable heart orgasms or simply Delight beyond delight. One of the earliest came when I was slightly over two, my father carrying me in his arms to the hospital to be operated on for a burst appendix. It was night and as I looked at the stars with incomprehensible wonder, I felt milk flowing from the heavens, joy beyond words.

Another happened when I was about seven and a man came to a hotel in the Catskills where we were staying. A beggar who put a hat on the lawn, taking out and putting together a wooden instrument with silver keys. When he played, I did not know what hit me, my sense of life transformed in an instant. He played Jewish songs that opened the heavens and my heart and I knew I must learn to play the clarinet.

As a child I began to realize there was a spectrum of experience beyond the ordinary, in which life could feel more than life—or, rather, life revealed just how alive life could be. There is a rose and there is a Rose! There is life and there is Life!

When I was seventeen and kissed Laurel goodnight, inner stars lifted me and I danced all the way home. By the time I was nearing thirty I was learning how to distill this glow and work with it, a beautiful work that lifts one all life long (Eigen, 2014c).

So many kinds of O-moments. I have worked with individuals who went mad and felt that was the most orgasmic experience of their lives, packed with extremes of horror–bliss. For some, rage is orgasmic (Eigen, 2002). Many tell of an orgasmic thread running through and peaking in psychedelic experiences, the opening of heart, psyche, and universe reaching past the nameless. In psychotherapy, one meets many individuals who cling to destructive experience as a way to heighten self-experience, sometimes an addiction to failed birth, whip as umbilical cord.

The love–death theme has a long history in life and literature, a peak moment in Wagner (e.g., *Tristan and Isolde*), whose Jew-hatred found magnified echoes in Hitler's blood lust, a nearly orgasmic decimation of Jewish people and other beings judged inferior, contaminating the super-race. It is not hard to see an orgasmic element in Hitler's rhetoric, demeanor, and celebration of German purity fed by cruel pleasures.

There are many ways of seeing love–death themes, including links with an ancient narrative of transformation involving death–rebirth, for example, the crucifixion–resurrection of Jesus and the older mystery cults of Egypt and Greece, in which the initiate would be sealed in a cave mimicking burial and be reborn with the rise of the solar god at dawn. It is said that Jonah died in the whale and was reborn three days later by his ejection. A phrase in French calls orgasm a "little death". One must lose the self to find the self is one of many formulae that participate in this archetype with wide application.

An especially colorful, intense variation is found near the end of *The Zohar* (Liebes, 1993; Matt, 2009). Rabbi Shimon, a hero of *The Zohar*, calls an assembly on the day of his death, an assembly at which only he will speak. He plans to reveal any remaining secret that he can but finds, near the end, he must not do so. What happens instead is that his death day becomes his wedding day.

He announces he has never been married until now. This, of course, was not literally so. He lived a sanctified married life and one of his grown sons was at his side at that moment, relaying his words to a larger audience as the master spoke. What he disclosed was that today he would marry the Shekinah, God's feminine presence, the Holy Spirit (to my mind, a kinship with Shakti, Shakti–Shekinah as sisters). A complete marriage that happened with the kiss of Shekinah at the moment of his death. Kiss of death? Kiss of life? A transformation that goes on and on, in one dimension an unending psycho-spiritual orgasm, in others serene bliss, joy, ecstasy, and that most elusive reality, part of Israeli–Muslim greetings: peace. Tumult, transcendence, incarnation, cooking in the great cauldron of experience.

In a wonderful Brazilian film directed by Marcel Camus, *Black Orpheus*, the love couple is followed by Death at carnival. The love couple succumbs to the inevitable, suffering loss of personality, self, life, and one feels a sad quiescence at the end of this extended, muted orgasmic flow, more a race with Death, suffused with arresting music. The film ends with the rising sun, dawn, new life, children, music, much as in a Shakespeare play (life goes on) or Walt Disney film (the sunlight after the storm).

The awesome musical, *The Gospel at Colonus*, the Oedipus story played by an all black cast featuring a gospel group, The Blind Boys of Alabama, had a scene towards the end, after Oedipus went through his own version of torment–resurrection, and as he is rising from the grave of his life, the singers chant, "Higher, higher, higher." My breath stops and tears come as I feel it today, more than thirty years later, a climactic moment in theater. The rise of the human soul through the torments of hell we go through here on earth, a coming through.

In *Coming Through the Whirlwind* (1992), I depict different kinds of rebirths, some monstrous. There is a moment in the *Bhagavad Gita* when Krishna reveals himself in his true monstrous form, too much for a human to bear. Lurianic Kabbalah (Eigen, 2012, 2014a,b) tells the story of vehicles that God uses for creation breaking under the strain of divine energy, our job being to be partners in repair of the ruptured universe, our own capacities, and divine powers. A divine orgasm too much for the divine body to take. A basic theme in Bion is the problem of building tolerance for intensity of experiencing and use of capacities (Bion, 1970, 1990, 1994; Eigen, 1998, 2011, 2012). It is not difficult to imagine why we are such self-confusing beings, afloat in so many multi-directional complexities.

There seems to be a double set of attitudes with regarding death. We will come through it, we will not. Death as end and opening. We have eternal moments now and death moments now. We are fallible, fragile, injured in all kinds of ways. There are healing processes that often work but also do not work. A man gets cancer nine years ago and thinks the treatments have beaten it, only to discover suddenly that his life expectancy is a few months. Bion was returning to India in old age for the first time since childhood, only to discover he had leukemia and he died in England without reaching his goal. His wife describes scattering his ashes in Norfolk, amidst land and sky and waters he loved. How is it one feels, even in the scattering of ashes, an uplift of spirit, a sense of the whole of a life of a man who gave it all he could.

Here are a few words by Francesca Bion (1995) about their stays at Norfolk:

> During the sixties we spent holidays in Norfolk where we had a cottage on the North coast. Bion infected the children with a love of that area known to him since boyhood, and had visited often during the twenties and thirties. The bracing climate and austere landscape were very much in tune with his temperament. We all remember vividly the fascinating country walks, the endless supply of beautiful churches to explore, ice-cold swims, lark song, primrose picking – and he made it all precious with his deep fund of knowledge and reminiscences. He particularly enjoyed painting there; its clear air and wide skies make it a painter's paradise – provided you can prevent the easel from being blown away by the constant wind.

Why is it, for me at least, such a conclusion opens something inside. I have sometimes had experience of a person after death more real in some way than when I knew him. What is this life after death that sometimes can have more Life? A Taoist I once read said, "There is only Life." Such a manifestly absurd remark ripples and grows as one gets into it.

What were people thinking when they were sealed in the Death Pit of Ur, a Queen and her living retinue? And the robbers who entered and pillaged it two hundred years later? Bion felt a monument should be erected in honor of the plunderers as early scientists who opened doors to history and a fuller sense of humankind. The thrill and terror of opening an old tomb—that begins to sound something like psychoanalysis. There is perhaps a door that never opens. But there is, too, one that never closes, never stops O'ing.

CHAPTER SEVEN

Just beginning: ethics of the unknown

There has always been one or another form of human therapy. Evidence suggests this was so when we lived in caves. People have been trying to cure physical and mental pain from time immemorial. Since ancient and perhaps pre-ancient times there have been healers.

I think psychoanalysis makes a contribution, adds to the pool, by calling attention to psychic realities, touching details of what goes on within oneself and between patient and therapist, new forms of interaction. I do not know that there previously existed such a nuanced sense of self–other interweaving and exploration, experiencing experience and investigating it as it happens moment to moment and over time, hot off the psyche. Wordsworth's "emotion recollected in tranquility" might be a hint, but he was referring to the poet's relationship to himself and his writing. In therapy we have co-creative partners discovering tastes of relationships with oneself and others *in vivo*. Harold Bloom outrageously claimed Shakespeare invented the "human" as we know it. I am tempted to claim Freud invented the psyche (a term from antiquity). Or, at least, ways of apprehend-ing psychic life with additional color, flavor, scent, and significance.

Two people in the room waiting on the emergence of unknown emotional reality, everything expressible. Freud noted that all kinds of emotions one dare not feel while awake can find expression in dreams, partly because one is safely lying in bed and will not act on them. In a way, therapy is akin to a waking dream, inviting communication of wounds, scars, and potential, without physical injury. A situation in itself with potential for building tolerance of experiencing, a kind of implicit psychic gymnasium.

Freud made a catalogue of internal danger signals, anxiety, shame, and guilt among them. He labeled many kinds of anxiety, for example, birth anxiety, separation and abandonment anxieties, castration anxiety. Since Freud, the list has expanded. One thing psychoanalysis finds is that we are phobic about our own minds. We can posit other worlds but a lot can be gained by associating fears in the night with mental dread. Our minds or psyches or souls populate boundless, amorphous night with what we put in people during the day. We are a repository of age-old trauma, catastrophic happenings and fears. Good feeling competes with bad, a balance that shifts and sometimes places us in jeopardy. One thing therapy can do, depending on luck, circumstance, and skill, is shift the balance for the better. Even a little can go a long way.

Bion feels that psychoanalysis is embryonic and that there is an embryonic aspect of the human psyche. There have been proliferations of "schools" of psychoanalysis and psychoanalytically related, derived or informed therapies. New movements continue to this moment. I have gained from all of them that I have had contact with. I feel wars between groups is more territorial and political or economic than knowledge based. Parochial wars are based on narrowing the field of possible knowledge to sectors that have been carved out, hands on the elephant. We might not know how they fit together or are mutually nourishing. But that does not nullify the positive contributions each can make. No matter what claims one makes, psychotherapy involves sensing and feeling one's way into work with oneself and another with difficulties and roadblocks. There is no problem-free environment, inner or outer, for human beings.

Uncertainty is so much a part of this work that Bion (1970) called the psychoanalytic attitude Faith, which he, partly, described as being without memory, expectation, desire, or understanding. Radical openness to present impact and response. He would say, if you think you are seeing the same person, you are seeing the wrong person. At times, he would say that about changes from moment to moment in the session itself. What changes have you and the patient undergone since the latter entered the room? Can one ever catch up to the "what"? One works with the uncatchable. Notations Bion used for this situation: F in O, T in O. Faith in the face of unknown reality. Transformations in unknown reality. To paraphrase a Bion saying, it is not a matter of knowing O, but being O (Eigen, 2004b, p. 124, 1998, 2012).

This is a far cry from words in psychoanalytic institute catalogues emphasizing understanding. It is much closer to Freud's "free-floating attention" and "free association". Neither may be "free" but an open attitudinal direction is set as a challenge. Surely there is growth in understanding, but something more, deeper, fuller, harder to pin down linked with quality of experiencing, a feel for life (Eigen, 2004d, Eigen & Govrin, 2007). It seems safe to say no one is without expectation, memory, understanding, and desire. Bion describes an impossibility as the path of psychoanalysis. In one's own way, one senses the possibility of a shift of attitude and emphasis, a field of practice, a path of growth. In particular, growth of a capacity Bion points to. Bion's work is an avenue of access and aid to cultivating the openness to experiencing he touches. To accept this challenge is a humbling act of respect and care for psychic reality that necessarily requires leaving room for the unknown in others and oneself.

In practice, I often reach a deep point of not knowing, a kind of creative waiting, that shifts the ambience of the room. As time goes on, a person with me begins to sense something further, perhaps a still point of her own that is a little freeing. It is less a matter of solving problems on their own terms as shifting the center of gravity, allowing something more to grow.

On one level the notion of unknown emotional reality is a hypothetical construct. On another, it is a sensed, living reality. Isn't unknown emotional reality real for you?

There is an ethics of the unknown. An attitude of unknowing leaves things open, protects against false omniscience. In an argument with your partner, you might be convinced that you are right, the other wrong. It is commonplace to blame the other, exonerate the self. The reverse also is not unusual. Aggression turns against the other and/or the self. If we assimilate the fact that we do not know everything about ourselves and the other and that, like the universe, we are mostly unknown, a sense of humility and openness might have a chance to grow. We may become more interested in learning more about who we are and readying for further development. This is an entirely different attitude than slamming the door with dogma.

The possibility of a more exploratory appreciation of complexity is an old concern. Socrates taught that much of what passes for knowledge is opinion and that we are victimized by our self-celebratory tendencies. In my book, *Rage* (2002), I write that the sense of being "right" has done more harm in human history than any other attitude. It is even used to justify murder. Self-idolatry goes deep and it is hard to break out of the right–wrong trap. One might not have answers but might be able to share a response. With luck, good will, persistence, and care (not to mention skill and experience), fields of impact-response grow.

When I began practice, what came to be called "borderlines" exploded on the scene. What to do with raw sensitivity, reactivity, sensitive anger, sensitive wounds. You could be in the middle of what seemed like a productive conversation about important concerns when, without warning, a hole in the earth opened and you dropped into it, a hole your patient told you about but now you knew first hand.

For years, the literature was filled with issues about borderline anger. At some point, it dawned on me that a function of that anger was to peck the response system needed by the patient into being. A growth in psychic sensing was needed. Now, many therapists feel at home with so-called "borderlines." Not that it is easy, but they tend to "know", that is, "sense", what to do because the response system to work with this level of wounded, angry sensitivity has begun to develop. A spontaneous, long-term growth of psychic sensing and know-how was called into being by insistent reaction to injury.

At this moment of history, something similar has to happen with problems related to psychopathy. The term "psychopathy" is not used anymore. It has been changed to "sociopathy." Maybe both terms should be used, pointing to social and psychical aspects of loss of feeling for others in the process of trying to get what one thinks one wants. Many years ago, we were taught that psychopathy had to do with defective conscience. I would emphasize lack of sensitive caring about the feelings of others one injures. In our success-oriented world, getting ahead is more important than worrying about what happens to others as one moves along. One's own success and survival is what counts. This attitude, a kind of psychopathy of everyday life, is endemic in individuals and the larger social scene.

When I was younger, I was taught that you cannot analyze a liar. Analysis was about truth and analyst and patient alike were in pursuit of it. That may be so. But lying is also ubiquitous, part of how consciousness works. And if you cannot analyze a liar, you cannot analyze anyone. Especially since a liar is also doing the analyzing. This is a challenge that exercises us today.

The resilience and resistance and well nigh universality of psychopathic tendencies is knocking on our door, knocking on our psyches and, one hopes, in time will stimulate response systems to meet it. Is psychic sensing enabling work with psychopathy growing in the wings? Can we sense it, help mediate it, grow with it? It will not mean we will become lie-free beings. We can no more stop lying than breathing. But there could be ways we can learn to sense and work with our amazing lying resourcefulness in less destructive ways. Affective attitude plays a role in how capacities are used. It may be no accident that we are in an Age of Psychopathy *and* an Age of Sensitivity (Eigen, 2004d, 2006a).

As noted above, psyche is more unknown than known. If we think we know only a little about a small portion of the matter of the universe, how much less do we know about psychical reality? Bear this in mind when you get drawn into wars between "schools" and disciplines, with all their contributions and limitations. Paradoxically, realization of such immensity can be freeing as well as paralyzing. If you do not think that what you do is the all of everything, you may be freer to give your all to it.

From my earliest days in the field, I felt a sense of practicing at the margins and a sense that psychoanalysis was a marginal formation in our economic age. Yet, I felt at the center of things, that I was contributing from the inside. Psychoanalysis brought me close to the center of life, my life, my attempts to live life. It permeated me and gave me tools to work with. More, it grew and changed with me, as if we were both babies learning to live and live together, a daily creative process. Today, in our offices, we may do something, feel or say or think something that will, over time, make a difference in life lived.

CHAPTER EIGHT

Life kills, aliveness kills

In my view, a lot can be done with the life drive before getting to a death drive. Life kills. Aliveness kills. I have seen people die from too much aliveness. Susan Deri used to tell of a case diagnosed as "chronic schizophrenia". Her patient, with support, eventually lived in an apartment and supported himself. This in itself took many years. But he was not satisfied with self-maintenance. He wanted love. His own analyst did not have a fulfilling love life and she feared for him. One day he came in and told Susan that he was in love and his loved one loved him. Susan was incredulous, sat at the edge of her seat, held her breath, expressed happiness through her alarm. He spoke of his joy, married, and died of a heart attack on his honeymoon. Among many "explanations" and imaginings, one cannot help thinking that happiness was too much for him and the increment in aliveness killed him. One needs to build resources to support aliveness, no easy matter (I write about this case and other transitions between aliveness–deadness in *Psychic Deadness*, 2004c).

The life drive is not wussy. It is allied with desire and aggression. One kills to eat, injures to gain and secure territory, competes for mates. Predator–prey relations are on the side of life, death as a result of appetite and need. In human social life, ambition takes over this function and skyrockets. Traditionally, Eros is allied with disturbance, war, rage, injury, as well as intense satisfaction. The Western literary canon begins with the word Rage, Homer's story of war as the result of erotic theft. It did not take Freud to point out that human beings are inept at handling life forces or ins and outs of difficulties with aggression and passion (Eigen, 2002, 2006b).

Today, our economic system is fused with the taste of power and feeds on its own ambition. Henry Kissinger called power an aphrodisiac, a kind of life drive gone wild. For the sake of gain, it destroys—poisons air and water and land and psyche. The life drive, once productive, once in service of survival, has itself become a menace, a threat to life. There is enormous resistance or incapacity or unwillingness to take in and work with what we are doing—*denial of violence* inherent in our sense of life. Addiction to gain, dominance, power promotes more addiction to gain, dominance, and power and inability to let in and counteract negative effects of this spiral contributes to its momentum.

Attached to this cycle is fear of the psyche. As if letting in psychic awareness would be suicidal to one's ambitions. As if letting in awareness of a fuller psychic reality would undermine one's desire or, at least, slow one down. Epidemic child abuse and suicide are among discountable side effects of the lust for power. Economic mania discounts many kinds of violent offshoots of its activity, justified by "self-interest", a psychopathy of everyday life (Eigen, *Age of Psychopathy*, 2006a, http://tinyurl.com/yal4wth).

Below are psychological factors that play a role in maintaining the *status quo* and enabling it to mushroom. Until we, as a human group, are able to build resources to work with our feelings (Eigen, *Feeling Matters*, 2006c), no amount of social reform will be sufficient. The problems listed are endemic to human nature, family, groups, individual, national, organizational.

1. Fear of the psyche, of emotional reality.
2. Belief one knows what reality is, including emotional reality, with consequent defensive stance with regard to one's system, emotional/mental/social.
3. Hatred of the complexities of growing emotionally in a fuller way. Insofar as material growth is substituted for emotional growth, the psyche to handle material expansiveness fails to exist.

4. Habit—easy targets—children are easy targets, so are spouses—they are near at hand, exert pressure, cause stress, bring out the stress fractures in one's personality. Inability to tolerate frustration of close impacts, or perhaps most impacts that challenge one's rigid or shaky "homeostasis" (the way one has become organized as a person).
5. In my book *Rage*, I note that a sense of being "right" has caused more damage in history than most other attitudes. Robert Fliess early called attention to the sense of self-righteousness in the child abuser. A sense of being right justifies many kinds of violence. Being right to invade Iraq because of its weapons of mass destruction; being right to cleanse a child of a devil by beating the devil out of it; a sense of being wronged by one's spouse "justifies" rageful violence. The sense of feeling "right"—I am the only God, a possessive God, have no others before you, especially not yourself—is an important part of human nature. Often, perpetrators are traumatized traumatizers who fear encroachment, seek to even the score, "right" things. This "right", I think, has a delusional aspect which mates with hallucinating something negative about the other that needs "righting". It is a tendency that may be built into personality, mind, cells, a kind of rigid–fragile neural "homeostasis". It is also part of the national rhetoric, part of the "we".

    Another piece of "delusional hallucinating" I found in some rape perpetrators was that they felt the person they raped was loving them (the people of Iraq would cheer us as heroes). These rapists imagined being loved for their violence, which they felt was an expression of fusional need. They experienced what they were doing, in some regard, as very soft and life giving. There are myriad variations of this story, this structure.
6. Premature jumping to action on the basis of very incomplete information or misinformation, or outright lies to support one's wishes, drives, needs, hopes, ambitions—whether individually or part of a group. In *The Psychotic Core* (2004a), I described this as "miscalculation from the viewpoint of omniscience": Thinking you know something you do not and pre-emptively acting on it. This was one of the horrible possibilities of the "cold war". Now we see outright manipulation of psychotic anxieties (annihilation fears, dread of loss) in high places, psychopathic manipulation of fear and anger on a large scale.

7. The need to be *numero uno*—which is a delusion. The need to maintain one's delusional system of being a certain kind of person with certain kinds of beliefs. Or the power of one's country *vis-à-vis* all other countries. A boss model, rather than a partnership model.
8. Economic political interests in the case of war, invasion, co-option of others' goods or properties in some way (melded in delusional, calculating fashion with ethical proscriptions such as thou shalt not steal, envy, covet, murder—ethical proscriptions used as a mask for doing exactly what is proscribed).

One wonders why real talk and work involving social and familial violence is off the mark, even off the table. Partly because addressing such violence would bring to the fore problems adhering to national violence, economic violence, which are whisked off center stage. Yes, but even if this were somehow addressed, the problem is ultimately one of our makeup, a psychical element, insufficiency in face of our emotional life. A perennial call for work and wonder, hope, regret, and care.

CHAPTER NINE

Mini-moments

Marin and I

Marin: I jumped out the window three times today. Saw seven times seven devils. Chewed a mango that imprisoned a toad. Did you ever eat a toad in a mango? A beautiful mixture of colors. And here I am with you. What did you do today? Anything exciting?

Mike: Marin, I saw the sea when I woke up. I saw the sea from my window and feared it was going to sweep me away. I feared drowning. Your day sounds better. But here I am with you now. We're both here. And there's forty minutes left to our meeting. Will we be here then too?

I often wonder what the end of a session will turn out to be, given its start. How one starts determines so much. That goes for life in general. The way one constitutes oneself at the beginning sets a course that widens and deepens in time. Yet I do feel there is room for new beginnings, that one is not totally stuck on the road on which one finds oneself. It is hard to reset oneself, to find a better starting point. There is much pressure against it.

Marin blinks at me. No, now I think she is just blinking. She is having a blinking fit. Is she doing this partly on purpose or is it just happening? Should I say something? Will I be nosy, intrusive, bothersome? I remember old films from childhood, words like blinking, blimey, parts of mild swearing, strong feeling, although not too strong. My own eyelids are slits, semi-shut, as if I am peeking out of a fortress afraid of an enemy. I often feel I am about to be attacked. I appreciate being with Marin. I like it a lot. We are both threatened creatures. It has taken years for us to reach this point, at ease with our threatened states together.

We look forward to sharing the little time of forty-five minutes a week together. We used to see each other five times a week the year she came out of the hospital when she began work with me. I call it work but I am not sure what it is, hanging out together. It is fun to have someone you like to hang out with. More than fun. It is a relief.

Part of the relief is we speak the same language. Neither of us is limited to the language we speak together. Each speaks other languages too with other people or just with ourselves, inside our very alone selves. I think that is another good thing we each share, how alone we are, *very* alone in some profound way. Was it Hegel who said only one person ever understood me and he did not understand me? Marin and I both feel this way. It is not all we feel, but we feel this too. That is another reason we like to be together. Neither of us makes the other upset about our aloneness. As Winnicott said, we are alone together, perhaps not quite the way Winnicott meant, but not too far away either.

Marin continues: I'm broken.

Mike: I'm broken too.

Marin: I doubt you're broken the way I am.

Mike: How are you broken?

Marin: I'm broken different ways on different days. Today I'm shattered green glass, a green bottle that was found in the earth when Con Ed men were digging near the foundations of a building. They found a little blue bottle and a little green one. I'm the little green one. They gave me the bottle as a keepsake and it seemed very strong. I didn't think it would break. It slipped out of my hand and shattered on the sidewalk. There are pieces of me on the sidewalk, alive on the sidewalk. Like a segmented worm only they are not organic. They have no skin, no thing that bleeds if you step on them or cut them. Just pieces of glass that can cut you if you touch them the wrong way.

Mike: Am I the blue bottle I wonder? I don't feel much like a blue bottle today. Not too blue.

Marin: You don't have to be the blue bottle. I think the blue bottle is me being left out of everything, me all alone. And the green bottle is me shattered, all broken, shards.

Mike: Yes. I feel what you're saying. They're both important. They're both real.

Marin: I'm glad you said that they're real. They really are. To be really real is important to me.

Mike: To me too, although I often don't do a good job of it. I get scared of being too real.

Marin: I know. I've seen that. I scare you when I'm too real.

Mike: You're being very nice to me.

Marin: I have to keep you in good condition. Someday you may be less afraid of me.

In this case the session ended well, better than it started. I feel I was given another chance to do it better. We left our worlds in better shape than we found them, always a blessing. It does not always go this well. It was as if a deep meditation gong sounded inside and the ripples said that having another chance is part of living. That is part of what Marin and I are about, being broken and giving each other chances.

Impenetrable shatter

"Come to my apartment this instant or I'll throw myself through a window."

These were the words I heard when I answered the phone. I knew it was Devi and suicide was always a possibility. Sometimes, I say or think, "I hope you stay suicidal for a long time." Where there is life, there is . . .

I was taught not to help people become un-suicidal too quickly. Often a person is used to feeling awful if that is a chronic state. To rush into a better state without inner means to support it can be more harmful than going slow. Not that one has a choice. Things happen, one responds.

My mind instantly saw glass shattering. Shattering again. Continuous shatter. Mind shattering. The words that came out of my mouth were something like, "Ah, to shatter oneself and be free." I glanced around my office and saw glass everywhere. A mess to clean up. But comforted myself thinking it could be worse, it could be blood, body parts, brains.

When I came to, Devi was crying. "I can't. I can't." he sobbed over and over. I did not know if he meant he could not throw himself through the window or something else, a deeper can't. People often feel like a coward because they cannot do something they want to do and do not want to do, like kill themselves or change themselves.

"What is the can't?" I asked.

"The can't is I can't get past myself. I can't go through myself."

Long pause, his remarks registering on me and himself as well. I felt he was hearing himself. We worked a long time for the possibility of his saying something he could hear. Often, he would speak and it would go past him, bullets that missed.

There are so many stories of going through something, a rabbit's hole, a looking glass, a closet. Alice's going through led to a world of new torments, far from heaven. A bit like Hamlet's dilemma—would or would not death free him from pain? What does one have to go through to be free of pain?

"What would it be like to be free of oneself?" I asked. "Free of one's personality?"

"Where is your hell?" he asked.

"You can't see or hear it? You can't feel it?"

Was he tone deaf (tone death) to other people's hell? Maybe in some way. But I knew he could see—whether or not he felt it—he could see it.

"I see hell everywhere," Devi said.

"Our appointment is in two hours," I said. "Our next meeting in hell."

To say we had a lot to talk about would miss the point. We did not say much but we felt the thickness, an impenetrable density. Yet, it had weak spots, traces of soft spots, edges, filaments to pull a little. A dense tangle. We sat with it. For me it was a relief to see him—one more time. A relief to feel this thing that does not budge.

Where is your face?

"Did you see the photo of the woman's face torn off by a pet chimpanzee?"

I nodded but Garren did not wait for my nod. He was already high speed.

"My face has not been the same. It's gone. Torn off. I look in the mirror and don't see it. I see a mess of flesh, bones, nerves. There is nothing to me but gross, yucky horror."

He paused and I had a sense he was waiting for me to confirm his description of what he looked like. I thought of accounts I read about face disfiguration and operations to "correct" it. I knew from my own experience how distorted I can look or feel I look. I know that the face is the soul, what one says of the face one says of the soul. But this is not always so. When I was growing up, I would hear that how one looks is not the true measure of who one is. In high school, the adage applied to homely people who had good souls, although Shakespeare linked deformity of soul with body.

Now in my seventies, I have a hard time with such binaries. I gravitate to faces that are well used, textured with experience. When patients speak of envied beauty, I often feel out of it. Popular stars they mention do not do much for me. The face in front of me is usually good enough for me.

I wonder what I must look like to Garren. Torn face, torn soul. I look for signs of horror but find his lips downturned in something like disgust. Hard to tell the difference between disgust and gritting lips in tension.

"Are you pressing me out of you?" I ask. "Keeping me at arm's length?"

"Do you see you in me, me in you?" he countered.

I remember a similar look I had when I was younger. It was more a way I felt inside than looked outside. Holding myself tight, becoming a shield. Not only afraid of letting in toxins but fighting against toxins long entrenched. Disgust with—God only knows. I picture a baby tightening, fighting, going dead. He dreams of toxic waters and he is a fish unable to survive. Soon he will die or be crippled.

Disgust shuts out the bad taste of life. It keeps a lot of good taste out too.

> "I ripped a photo of our cat when I was a kid," said Garren. "Torn to pieces. I was a kind of chimpanzee then. Jealous maybe? But it was more. I was trying to rip a feeling out of me, a caring feeling. I loved the cat. How do you explain ripping a photo of what you love? Ripping love out of you. I know the black rule: you do to others what was done to you. But I did not entirely have all the love ripped out of me. Some survived. Feeling survived in a crippled kind of way. I didn't kill the cat. I once cut the heads off a row of roses and my father said, "What are you doing!" I didn't know. I froze. That's a part of it, always frozen. Something's frozen."

What I took as disgust was something frozen? Is chronic disgust a chronic freeze? But I might be seeing my face in Garren and he was moving with his own trajectory. He ripped a photo, not a cat. He ripped his feelings. His feelings ripped him. When we are wounded inside we often rip at the wound, trying to scratch it out. We try to get rid of pain by ripping at it. We have something inside that rips at ourselves, rips our insides out.

> "How much would I have to rip out before I could rest? No wonder the chimp blew me up. Being torn apart happened to me. I know that. You know that. We know I was torn to pieces. But what gets to me now is sighting a chimp *in me* tearing *me* to pieces. A chimp I loved, felt close to—a me-feeling, warm, intimate. And a me ripping the hell out of it. What am I tearing at? I don't want to be a pet chimp, a pet cat, a pet anything! I don't want to be a pet! I'm trying to tear the pet-me out of me!"

He looks at me, I at him. I wonder what we are seeing. We are both so aware of expressions. He smiles a little and sighs, "There's got to be a better way."

The look I called disgust disappeared for the moment and a whole other face appeared, Not torn or disfigured. An intriguing face, a bit bemused, sophisticated and sincere. I felt my own gripping thing loosen, that gripping thing that stops feelings from breathing. I rip him, he rips me. Life rips us. Then a moment of rest, a pause. A rest between seizures. A face one can say yes to.

Voice echoes

"What am I doing here? I could be home sleeping. It's a beautiful fall day. The leaves are filled with color. Why am I here? You called your office a cave. I could be in a world filled with colors."

"How colorless am I?"

"That's a good question."

"Finally, a good question."

"Don't be so smart-ass. Just because you have to sit here all day doesn't mean I do. You chose your fate. Don't get pissed at me because you can't be outside enjoying yourself."

"We choose our fates?"

"We don't? Fate happens? I chose to—I don't know how to put it any longer. What are names for it—breakdown, crazy, nuts, mad, psychotic, not able to function, not able to . . . I chose my hospital stays? I chose my medication? I chose you as a therapist? How did this happen? I've no idea. I don't even know how to call what I am—names are ugly, wrong, mean. Maybe there should be no name for it—IT. Names are ordering devices but they—well, spoil things. They spoil what is."

"Experience is more important than names. But how would we communicate? Experience to experience? Don't let language get in the way?"

"You have an inkling of it, an inkling. You are not hopeless—not entirely. There. Now I'm being smartass like you. No one knows what it's like except the one who it's happening to, unless it's happened to you too."

"So you don't choose it. It happens."

"Don't rub it in. It could happen to you."

"What if it's happening all the time to everyone but most don't notice or pay it mind?"

"What difference would that make? To me, it's almost all that's happening. Except for the leaves, the colors, the air. Since I'm coming here, there are changes. Most of the time you're not a devil or witch. Now a voice says, 'Clean up Newark.' No, that's not what it says. It says, 'Don't you think you should go clean up Newark?'"

"It's gone from orders to questions?"

"Well, this time. This time it was a question. It was put as a question. It is an order in disguise, maybe. Doesn't it sound like an order to you?"

"Reminds me of the way my mother might ask me to clean my room or help with the kitchen."

"I know what you mean. It feels so sneaky when someone does that. For my mother, it wasn't cleaning my room—well, that too actually. What bothered me more was—I don't know—her asking me wouldn't I want to do this or that.

"Wouldn't you want to . . .!!!!" Who was this 'you'. It took my 'you' away. It infiltrated. Don't you want to—it feels like poison coming into me. A year ago I'd see a witch rather than feel the poison. Makes me wonder what I'll feel about the poison a year from now."

"Am I poisoning you now?"

"Aren't we always poisoning each other? Isn't that the point?"

"So maybe the idea of cleaning has some sense? Cleaning oneself of the poison. Can that be done?"

"I think somewhat, not totally. That's a difference too. Last year it would have been total. All clean, all poisoned. Now I am with you and if we are poisoning each other it is not all we are doing."

Silence for a time.

"When I was a kid, Newark had a bad name. It needed cleaning up. The voice is assigning me an impossible task. Mayors have promised to clean up Newark a long time. I took night classes there at Rutgers. It wasn't so bad. I liked walking around, feeling the life. Newark was good for me. I felt alive there."

"And what about the name—new, new-ark. Having the kind of mind I have, I think of Noah's ark."

"I see where you're going. I wouldn't have thought of that. But you got the sense of what I was saying. Life, new life. After the Great Storm."

"Yes, and through the Great Storm."

"Yes, and with the Great Storm. One wouldn't want to clean the life out of Newark. An odd thing—not odd, new—I just didn't notice it before—the voice, 'Don't you think you should go clean up Newark?' Don't you want—don't you think—it could be an order. Don't you want! Don't think!"

"I once had a therapist that asked me repeatedly, 'What do you want?' When I was away from him I kept asking myself, 'What do I want?' One day, an answer came."

"What do I want? What do I want? The voice doesn't come from out there. A new thing about it is I hear myself in it. It's my voice too. It and I use each other as disguises. Infiltrate each other's costumes. It's me too. I do hear my I in the voice, part of It. I'm part of the voice, in it, with it."

"I hear your voice with your I in it echoing in my cave."

"Sometimes it's a magic cave."

Every morning

Stu: Every morning is the scariest morning in my life. Every night is the scariest night in my life.

Mike: Which is scarier?

Stu: Night because you see things that aren't there.

Mike: Like?

Stu: Witches, devils.

Mike: And day?

Stu: You see scary things that *are* there. Witches and devils in people. Someone looks at you and you see the scary thing. Not all people. Some yes, some no. Some look at you and you want more. Others terrifying and you try to shut it out.

It's not so simple to shut out. Inside there's a kind of camera lens that changes with what you're looking at. It takes pictures that stay. Good things, bad things.

Mike: Only your eyes, through your eyes?

Stu: Voices too, good voice, bad voice. Good is comforting, like sky colors inside. Bad voice tells you to hurt others or yourself. Push someone into the road or walk into the road yourself and get hit by a car.

Mike: Get hit?

Stu: You're saying that makes me think of getting hit when I was little. My father hit me. My mother was a good voice, my father bad. I did wrong things and got hit. I could look at my mother and feel softer, my father fear. Sometimes I looked up to him. He had a lot of life. One moment life force, one moment death force.

It's the scariest thing when I don't obey the bad voice. "Push that man into the road." "Walk in front of the cars." When I don't do that it threatens to torture me. Defenseless. Totally alone. A spirit hurls me across the room. The pain follows and finds me, invisible pain. I vanish but not enough. It threatens to torture me but something in me won't do it. I don't push anyone into the road. I don't get hit by a car. It promises if I did it, no more torture. But I'm too weak to do it.

Mike: Only too weak?

Stu: Too weak, not brave. If I were strong—

Mike: If you were strong you would kill?

Stu: Yes, that's what it says. And I would stop being punished.

Mike: But you can't?

Stu: I can't move.

Mike: It's OK not to move.

Stu: I get the feeling you are telling me it's OK not to be strong.

Mike: What kind of strength?

Stu: Killing strength?

Mike: Are there any others?

Stu: This may sound odd and I'm afraid to say, but when I am quiet, very quiet, and the bad thing goes away or lessens for a moment—I feel something that's not strong or weak. Just feels like you feel the way good weather can make you feel. You lie there or take a walk, lie in the grass looking up at the sky and for moments you are between bad things.

Mike: The moment between?

Stu: The moment between.

Mike: I feel tears coming.

Stu: I do too.

CHAPTER TEN

Leaving and the impossible place

Norm and Denise

"Denise called me. She wonders why we can't meet. Yet she doesn't ask me to and I don't ask her. We hint. We tantalize. But we don't do anything. I'm not sure how much we even want to. She doesn't want to come back into therapy. But doesn't want to break off our contact either. She tells me how unhappy she is with her husband. She makes me want to be with her."

Norm is a vibrant, well-meaning therapist who tries to do good work. He is dedicated and competent and fears he is heading for a fall.

He continues, "It's been six months since I heard from her, two years since I saw her." He paused, letting two years sink in. There were ethical guidelines saying after two years of not seeing each other, a former therapist–patient couple may make romantic contact.

Norm describes how beautiful she is, how much he wants her. He is tempted to think she will make up for everything. She will supply what is missing.

> "I know I'm crazy. She can't come through. The sex will not be what I hope. She will find me wanting. She will withhold herself, become sullen. No matter how good things are, they will not be good enough. They will sour. I don't mean that things can't match ecstatic vision. They *really* sour. As goodness begins, poisons build."

Norm speaks of the five years Denise was his patient. Throughout that time, he yearned for her, imagined sex, barely got through sessions. She spoke of her unfulfilled life and he would be tempted to blurt out, "I'll be the one. I'll make you happy. We'll find the *Summum Bonum* together."

Rationality saved him from the plunge. He could see ahead and *knew* it wouldn't work. She was indecisive, damaged, disabled. There could be moments, no long run. He would reach for an erotic jewel, but fall into an emotional swamp.

For years he heard her cut through relationships nearly as fast as they formed. She stayed with her husband for convenience, but was sure someday she would leave. She was never with anyone she wasn't already leaving. She scarcely had time for her children. She certainly had no time for herself.

> "I saw her as always leaving, especially leaving herself, never settling in. A kind of hovercraft hovering over self. You never knew which way she'd go, but you knew she'd be somewhere else. You think you see her in one place but she's already on her way to others, several directions at once, never landing, always maneuvering."

Norm felt *too* settled in, monogamous over twenty years, a totally devoted family man who takes fatherhood seriously. A devoted psychotherapist, proud of his profession, still searching, learning. Would he risk damaging everything for moments of fantasy bliss?

Sometimes, he thought an affair with Denise would not be so damaging. His profession and marriage would survive. Denise and he would take what they needed and move on. Wouldn't he be short-changing himself, Denise, and life if he said no? Wouldn't that be cowardly?

Denise was always moving away from herself, moving away from others, moving away from life. How could he think they would find life together? Wouldn't he get his head handed to him? He must be crazy to think it would be heavenly. Norm saw with clearest vision heaven loaded with hell.

He thought about ways he and Denise reach out–draw away, tendrils reaching, never touching. She calls, they talk, not meet. "She wants to keep it in *the impossible place*," Norm said one day, with an air of discovery. A discovery he made through her. She brought him to *the impossible place*.

Perhaps the idea that he could break through, pin her down, meet and have an affair—that they could actually be with each other—perhaps all of this was fantasy, something that could never happen, part of yearning. Perhaps all she wanted was to have this sometimes contact, not in, not out. Perhaps all she wanted or could do was keep them in *the impossible place*. Perhaps that is all they dared. The idea that they could *actually* meet was their crazy dream. They best not risk it. Rather, they hit on an amazing compromise, which prolonged their need for each other, without gain, without loss, poised in tantalizing sensation.

Norm discriminated, at least, four principal strands in his experience with Denise.

1. The eternal analyst–patient couple. They will be analyst and patient forever.
2. Lovers: Penis seeking its sexual counterpart. Soul seeking Divine Moment.
3. Asshole seeking destruction (trouble with wife, profession, family, self).
4. The impossible place. An area seeking exploration.

For some time, Norm chafed against his discovery, Denise's gift. He did not want to be in *the impossible place* (TIP). He railed against it, rejected it. TIP was a place he wanted to be out of, not go deeper into.

> "Maybe Denise is a destiny message," I said. "Whatever you do or don't do with her, she's opening something you'd rather avoid. It may be best to avoid it. But if you're called upon to undergo a certain kind of growth, you'd best learn how to undergo it."
>
> Critic I: "There's a silly statement for you. Therapist as oracle. Let it mean what you want it to mean."

Critic 2: "Are you sure there's such a thing as growth? If there is, can therapy be its vehicle? What on earth do you mean by growth? Or perhaps what you mean is not on earth?"

Critic 3: "Are you trying to ejaculate on the patient? Eject the patient?"

Imaginary M. E. 1. "I've grown through being in impossible places. This is as much a fact as a back pain. Not all impossible places are workable. Some simply hurt. But I *have* gotten something from dipping into impossible places and holding myself there as long as I could. What is growth? Not one thing, perhaps. Did Adam and Eve grow after eating the apple? Did they learn that impossible places exist? Did something in their sense of what it is possible to experience alter after discovering *the impossible place*? Is this a kind of growth or invitation to grow?"

Imaginary M. E. 2: "How could you know if *the impossible place* that hit Norm was worthwhile? What sort of TIP did he find?"

Norm: "My TIP begins with a fantasy of filling a gap in my marriage. A fantasy of filling a gap between the wished for woman and the woman I have."

Norm has terrific sex with his wife, the actual woman. But they fight a lot. They wear each other down. They hate each other. They frustrate each other. They are each other's worst critics. They love each other. They are bringing up children: worry, fatigue, blame, hope, craving—fear of going under with everything life piles on. He is making a living, she is mostly staying home. She is angry that he is away so much, he is angry that she does not work more. He wishes he could be at home more, she wishes she were making more money. They are doing the best they can.

Worth underlining: Norm and his wife are having real-life sex and sometimes the real-life sex is great. Real sex is not what Denise is needed for. She is needed for fantasy sex, including the fantasy of sex without injury to self. Norm and his wife are battle scarred. For them, real sex pushes its way through a history of mutual injury, mutual hostility, mutual blame, and a sense of deprivation. Sex shines through the wounds. Denise offers fantasy of bliss without wounds, at least not the daily kind that wear you down, the petty flare-ups that grind the spirit.

In a way, marriage is an impossible place Norm and his wife are working with. They stay with it. It has been grueling but has given them their life. There is something deep within they remember, a glow not entirely killed, a fantasy at the center that still has pulse.

Denise offers more fantasy, less gruel. But that is only apparent. Norm knows Denise does not have the staying power his wife has. His wife would not tolerate a marriage of convenience. She makes emotional demands, leads with her gut, refuses to make believe things are better than they are. She lives her truth as best she can. What is amazing is their marriage withstands emotional realities. It may be wobbling, hobbling along, but goes on after truth explosions.

Norm is very clear that the fantasy of Denise is not one that could withstand marriage or lead to marriage. It is a fantasy of bliss made up of ever-fresh erotic pulsations and everything life is not. Yet, it is real in its own right, something our mind produces, something important to our sense of existence. It is amazing to be the sort of creature for whom life creates fantasies beyond anything it can fulfill. Lovers outside marriage help sustain tastes of heaven.

For a time Norm swung back and forth, should he, shouldn't he, could he, can't he? Denise's calls were real. What they might do was real. Yet, their relationship seemed unreal. He could not push past a barrier of unreality.

It struck me he was postponing exploration. Norm could obsess forever. "*The impossible place* opens a field of experience to explore," I said. Denise may be a destiny message, but work in therapy might help decipher it. I do not merely mean cognitive deciphering, but feeling one's way into a new place. For Norm, TIP made its appearance as an erotic sub-region of being. But the quandary he was in might lead to further discoveries.

> "I'm pinned to something paradoxical, to have and not to have," said Norm. "What does Denise want? What do I want? What do we make of what's happening? I'm more loyal than Denise. She runs away. I know whatever I have in mind with her can't be brought into reality. We are toying with something I know is impossible. Whatever we have—however fantastic it may be—it can't be what I'd like it to be. Still, it might be more than enough for awhile.
>
> "My penis and soul could have satisfaction in reality. My idiotic asshole self too. These pleasures are assured. What we can do is a lot. But what I really want is a thing in my mind that is not possible to realize. Denise brings me to a place in my mind where fulfillment is not possible. Or

perhaps it is possible as an idea, a fantasy, an imagining. A kind of heaven within.

"I'm getting a glimpse of what you mean by urging me to explore *the impossible place*. You are telling me to find an internal switch. Denise pushes the button but the switch is inside. You are telling me *the impossible place* is worth paying attention to. You are not telling me to have an affair or not to have an affair. You are telling me to pay attention to myself.

"I hear Denise saying, 'Fall in love with me so I can break your heart.' Denise is telling me *the impossible place* is an eternal broken heart.

"Doesn't a broken heart have a history? My sense of Denise is identified with someone who betrays a child's love. This was her history, betrayal of love. Her love was smashed over and over. Her father left her, courted her, left her, put her down, made her feel horrible, aroused her love again. He treated her love cruelly, abused her love, wouldn't let it die, wouldn't give it satisfaction. He kept her love alive so he could keep wounding it, leaving it. Her mother screamed a lot, then vanished in depression, leaving Denise alone. Rage and aloneness fused with mother love.

"Mother came like a storm that was always leaving. Storming, leaving. Broken love, left love, broken love with nowhere to go, except to leave, and leave, and leave.

"My love would have to encounter its own destruction at the hands of someone who destroyed her loving self. When Denise said she wanted me to fall in love with her so she could break my heart, I said, 'The real problem is you need to fall in love with me and find your heart not broken.'

"This is my great fantasy, my maddening conviction. She needs to feel her own loving self without destruction. That, I feel, is the point: for her to feel her loving self in a more benign connection, not as a prelude to destruction.

"I do have capacity to love that's a little less damaged, that sparks hers, a love that contains a wish for repair. Still, there's something in me I need to repair, some sense of loss, incompleteness, death. I want to go back in time. I feel an ache for certain ways I felt when I was young. I can almost taste the way I felt, that almost unconscious state, a little like the promise invoked by Denise. In those days I had affairs almost unconsciously. I look at teens now. They wouldn't believe, it's hard to believe, what it's like ten, twenty years later, on the other side of a family. Denise has managed not to make it to the other side. She neither is nor is not a teen, but she hasn't added the other side either. She's had a family without having a family. But in me she evokes an old sense of promise, a nostalgia for something I tasted long ago. There's an almost unconscious sense of being that speaks to something purer than can remain alive.

"Romeo and Juliet die before they can be disillusioned. If they don't die, they're not Romeo and Juliet anymore, sweet, deluded souls, delusionally, deliciously beautiful. Can love be true and delusional at the same time? Love *is* true and delusional—both. Do they really love and see each other, two fifteen-year-olds? What *do* they see? What I wrote as an adolescent felt so true, real, so painfully honest. *The impossible place* looks different at different times, stays with us, deepens our sense of loss . . ."

There are therapist–patient couples who become lovers and do well. One woman told me, "I don't think anything else would have worked. We seduced each other but fell in love. Call it transference. Nothing else could have gotten me out of myself. The force of therapy closeness broke through my shell. I couldn't have been with someone otherwise. I couldn't open up. No one could get through."

A man told me, "I cry when I think of her. I can't believe I'm this happy. I cry with happiness." He is living with a former patient who left therapy with him because he would not become her lover. Finally, he broke up his marriage to be with her. His marriage died years earlier. His wife was obsessed with business and chores. Feeling contact was replaced by anxious, hostile worry. He did not doubt his wife's love, but the controlling, anxious form it took killed love. After much soul-searching and agonizing, he reached out to one whose feelings reached him.

But there *is* a difference for Norm. Passion still lives between his wife and him. He hates his wife's controlling, anxious ways and she hates his controlling, anxious ways. But they, also, live from their emotional centers. Real nourishment seeps through, they fight and expel each other but let each other in too. They want more and wish it were better.

Norm doubts his patient's staying power. He is nearly certain that once he opens up she will draw away. He is convinced she needs heightened moments that nearly reach fulfillment, only to fall away, dissolve into longing and start up again with someone else. His mental calculus sees more to lose than gain by giving into temptation, although there is loss either way. The opposite is true for the other therapist–patient couples mentioned above. Their mental calculus concluded there was more to lose by not taking the leap. They leaped into more life. Norm feared giving up what wounded goodness he had for a doubtful bit of heaven that might be hell in disguise.

Yet, every half year or so, Denise calls. Their situation reminds me a little of Keats' Grecian urn, lovers never quite touching, always reaching. Leaving is reaching. Denise got something out of therapy and senses she has not used up what it offers, although she cannot quite take it further.

Lou

> Lou speaks of a different kind of leaving. "I left myself a long time ago and maintain a kind of contact by being judgmental. Judging others brings a kind of comfort. I'm on top, looking down, feeling safer, less threatened. A sense of superiority gives me an edge, makes me a cut above. I've become a kind of monster. My mind's a monster. I'm aware of it ticking off judgments all the time, tainting everything. I can't bear it, not a moment's peace. It's a crazy way to make contact. It cuts me off."

Lou grew up in a judgmental atmosphere. His parents put down friends, relatives, the world, life. Nothing Lou did escaped a caustic remark. His father yelled at him when he hurt himself and disparaged him if he did well. His mother found things wrong with anyone who called him. No one was good enough for Lou and he wasn't good enough for himself. Nothing escaped negativity. Lou vowed he would not be like them when he grew up. He would be sane, life loving, accepting, caring.

Lou worked hard and carved a niche for himself in life. He was dedicated to job, community, and family and became the kind of person he hoped to be, but in middle age began to falter. After weathering a series of financial and health setbacks, he noticed his thought process was becoming more virulent. He feared being bitter like his parents, something he fought against all his life.

Actually, the caustic side of his personality never had been fully suppressed. He worked hard at becoming a "nice" person and thought most people saw him as nice. He used his bitter aspect to make fun of people's faults and life's foibles, but did it in what he believed was a charming way, enlisting the sympathies of others.

When he was nasty, he was "cute." When he was "truthful," he imagined he was loveable. In early phases of therapy, he spent a good deal of time wondering why people did not call him or return his overtures.

As therapy wore on, Lou came to see the judgmental streak of his parents working in him like an acid corroding his life. It was part of his being he tried to control by charm, wit, hard work, and love, but it took its toll. He stared long and hard at his parents' judgmental quality and saw the hurt and hate they poured into it. They had hard lives, filled with injury and defeat. Their love was sour and rageful. In the end, Lou could not divorce himself from the emotional diet he was reared on, although he valiantly tried to transcend it, at least not be done in by it.

It is dreadful to discover that in fighting evil one may cut off sources of nourishment. In fighting parental rage, bitter injury, self-pity, Lou was in danger of losing love fused with it. He was nourished by a toxic situation and by fighting the latter he risked losing the former (Eigen, 1999). A lot of love goes into parental poisons. It took a long time for Lou to see that people reacted to him a little like he did with his parents: they did not want to take in poison with love.

> In a way, Lou came to therapy to collapse. Of course, he was collapsing anyway. But therapy gave him a place to finally let down. "I think I've been in a state of shock all my life, deeply frozen, out of play. But I've thrown myself into life as best I could. I did well until recent years. I don't know exactly what broke me down. Losing money was part of it. When everyone was making money in the stock market, I managed to lose. It was like losing blood. I never managed to get it right. It was like I *had to* lose. My heart attack changed everything. I've never been the same. All the hate I held back seeps out. There's nothing I can do about it. I feel the bitterness and the hate oozing out of my pores. I'm just like my parents—except I don't want to be like them. I never wanted to be like them. But now I see I'm at war with myself and it's breaking me apart."

When Lou spoke about a lifelong state of shock, he pointed to his chest, his heart. It was as if his heart broke or froze but some bit of consciousness rose above it. When he spoke of malicious judgment, he pointed to his head, the evil eye. "The center of me froze in shock but slivers of me rose to my head and behind my eyes. I became very critical of myself and others. I could spot weak spots and be cute about put-downs. For a long time, I got away with it, but the leakage finally mounted. The acid seeped down for years and now I can feel the sour taste all through me."

Sometimes, when Lou described his brain as a judgment machine, I recalled the sorcerer's apprentice, water rising against will: what one fights against proliferates. With the sorcerer's apprentice, flooding–drowning seemed to be the primordial threat. Lou described shock–freezing as primordial psyche stopper. Perhaps the two are related. Shock might defend against flooding, or types of flooding can grow out of shock. In Lou's case, negative judging threatened to flood brain, while heart remained in shock.

This was not the whole picture, since Lou also had a loving heart and clear mind. But shock and flooding imperiled them and brought him to the edge of physical and mental collapse.

While Lou was expressing the dread his breakdown precipitated, he discovered a book by Bion (1977) in my waiting room and picked up the notion of being without memory, expectation, understanding, and desire. The idea quickened him and he began obsessing about it. "Judging doesn't let me be without knowing. Judging is a way of controlling. Bion is talking about being open, without control. An open state of faith. Is it possible? I'm too anxious. I've got to stay in control. Judging controls contact. It's a way of making contact by cutting contact, so things don't get out of hand.

"Judging isn't all bad. I get into myself with it. I cut into myself. How would I be in contact with myself otherwise? Judging gets me in deeper. It's a crazy intense way of being me.

"Now judging is out of control and I fear the way it is aimed at my daughter. It's always been aimed at her. When she was an infant I worried she was not normal and now, in her teens, I take everything as a sign. If no one calls her and she doesn't have anything to do one weekend, I take it as a sign that something is wrong with her or me or her mother or all of us. A stigma. No one wants us; we're beyond the pale. My mind goes nonstop. She's no good, something awful about her, about me, my wife, we've done everything wrong. There is something horrible about us and my daughter getting no calls proves it."

What Lou describes is excruciating. Being without desire, expectation, or knowing would be a relief. His mind becomes a curse. A friend of his daughter's calls. She is moving to another city. What good is a call from someone who is leaving? His daughter needs friends who are here. Whatever happens, he calculates angles that make him discontent. "My mind persecutes me. It doesn't allow me to be. I need to ward off unpredictability. My parents could shock me, horrify me. You're too silent. They're too loud. You don't say enough but the result is the same—lack of contact.

"My friend, Y, is better than me. She's less judgmental. See, I'm judging. It's ubiquitous. I'm judging about not being judgmental. Why would you want to be with me? Others are less envious. In a dream, a guy shoots me before I shoot him. He's my judging self. The judging mind beats all my other thoughts to the draw. Maybe trying to shoot him isn't the best approach. Maybe I've been going about it the wrong way. Maybe returning shot for shot isn't the answer.

"I'm feeling terrible. Don't know what I can do. I'm too nasty for you? Not nasty enough? Maybe you feel hurt? Maybe you want me to agree with you? Argue with you? Maybe I should be this way, that way? It keeps on going. I judge my judging. But with you I feel something else growing. It's hard to describe but I feel a kind of accepting. I think that's the new thing that's coming out of this. Accepting my judging instead of fighting it. Is that possible? Judging is a kind of fighting, a constant fight mode. Now I feel a nascent clearing and can't believe it is happening. A taste of relief from a distance. Now it is closer. Something is changing. I'm feeling better and didn't expect to. I have qualities that are off. So does Y. Maybe we each have something to give. I'm constantly seeing who is better or worse. A terrible floating mind. How can somebody help me with this? Yet I feel something is happening, something I didn't anticipate. It seems obvious—but feeling it is a surprise. My mind ticks off all this bad stuff but there is more to me. Much more."

Lou did not like my quietness. I spoke but it was not the sort of speaking that overstuffed him. My being more in the background let him go through a series of states until a real shift occurred. His parents bombarded him. He bombarded himself, his wife, his daughter, his friends. He tried to bombard me into bombarding him. He needs overstimulation to feel alive and his sardonic behavior was "designed" to get a reaction out of people. Perhaps his "nastiness" is not only a way to get a reaction out of people, but also a way to somehow circumscribe or put the brakes on over-stimulation, thus placing some limit on flooding. The grim irony is that this way of reaching aliveness is swallowed by a deeper state of shock.

Frozen shock acts as a black hole gorging on stimulation. As soon as stimulation approaches the point of shock, it goes dead. My speaking more would feed the numbness. Nevertheless, Lou did feel me feeling him, which enabled him to feel himself.

The shock of ourselves and challenge of aliveness

In unconscious transformational grammar, leaving can mean its opposite. For Denise, leaving is a way of connecting. Leaving Norm is a prelude to reconnection. Breaking connection is part of maintaining connection. Her capacity for bonding was damaged in such a way that the only way she could maintain a relationship was by being on the way out of it. She needed to be on the way out to be some degree in.

Out becomes identical to in. Leaving becomes identical to staying.

Norm experiences Denise's leaving as an invitation to approach, as part of allure, yet knows approach will shatter as leaving is built into it. He learns through Denise that leaving can be an approach that goes on endlessly, that it is possible to make contact by refusing contact.

Norm ruefully appreciates aspects of his marriage more by envisioning what might or might not happen with Denise. The erotic lure promises to repair damaged capacity for contact and is heavenly in its own right. But actual "leaving" tendencies are more incarnate in his marriage. His wife and he leave each other on a daily basis in a multitude of ways, especially by disagreements. Leaving is built into their staying. In order to get along better they will have to learn how to modulate the need to pull away, to differ, to fight, so that it is not so devastating. Room has to be made for freer flow of leaving–staying tendencies.

For Lou, judging as a way of severing is a way of connecting. Judging = cutting = connecting. Lou tries to be extra nice to cover mental cutting. The opposites, nice and cutting, not only become parts of a system, but fuse. Lou feels life spin out of control as niceness becomes one with cutting himself and others to pieces. The more he tries to connect with himself and others, the more severing–severed he becomes.

Therapy provides an atmosphere that absorbs his cutting capacity to hyper-judge. It gives him room to spin himself out, find and have faith in the more in him. Therapy allows Lou to recover from himself. Some patients need a good fight. With Lou, I am relatively resistance-less, a kind of resilient nonresistance. This gives him a chance to live with, take in, and absorb aspects of the grisly logic that takes over his life: if cutting is a way of connecting, connection is cutting. In fact, that is precisely the way he describes his early life with parents, a series of explosions, shocks, cutting gestures and remarks. For Lou, connection was, indeed, cutting, and cutting a way to connect. Insofar as this logic goes unchecked, destruction spirals.

Lou tried to cut damaging explosions and shocks with his mental judgment machine, but could not stop injuring himself in the process. One of therapy's perennial challenges is working at the point where self-injury becomes confused with self-care. In Lou's case, tools he used to "cure" himself were versions of what originally injured him. To fight damage with damage takes one only so far. Lou got worse and worse until, finally, he reached for something else.

When things go well enough, leaving–staying work together. Relationships combine both tendencies in variable ways. Even when leaving and staying are well coordinated, there are areas or ways in which they become fused, reversible, and equivalent. There are points at which leaving means staying, staying means leaving. History may play up or down identities and reversals. But the capacity for leaving to mean itself and its opposite can be bafflingly poignant. The shock of ourselves is perennial. We are challenged by our own aliveness.

CHAPTER ELEVEN

Giving it a try

"I've come for help but don't expect any. I've always been miserable and it's getting worse as I get older. When I was young I thought it would go away. Now I feel it will always be with me. It's like I swallowed a lot of mud and it is dragging me down."

Gerry watched me carefully, quizzically, as if he expected me to understand completely and not at all.

"I thought I knew what down was. I didn't have a clue. No matter how down I go, the more I can go. There's no end to down. And yet I can't be all the way down, so far down that I can't speak. I'm trying to reach you, to get something from you that will help me. I'm not totally sealed—yet."

"Not totally," I resonate. "Not totally is important."

"I once hoped to get totally better and maybe in my heart of hearts I still hope I do. But I doubt that is likely. Maybe all I should hope for is a little better, although I'd like a lot better."

"How much would be enough, do you think? What should therapy offer?"

"A little more than a little, " said Gerry questioningly, looking at me looking at him.

"In how short a time?" I wondered aloud.

"Hmmm. That's a tough one. I've been depressed forever. How long should it take to get a little more than a little less depressed? How about two months, doc? Can you do it in two months?"

"I'm glad it's not totally," I continued. "Totally is not too likely. That takes *some* pressure off. But two months?"

"The first time I took medication I felt better faster than that. But it didn't last. I've been on medication for many years. Doctors try different meds and doses. Some work better but problems come. I get heavy, lose sexual interest, feel "funny". At first I felt more me, then more not me. I get scared of what I might do to myself. I feel more despairing because what's supposed to help almost does and doesn't. Once you feel better, it's a longer way down."

"It's easier to stay down if that's what you're used to?"

"Yes, easier than raising and dashing hope."

"And therapy?"

"It's helped but hasn't solved anything. I've had a number of therapists. They tried but there's only so much you can do. Words sink in the darkness."

"Why should it be different now?"

"I don't know. Maybe it won't. Do you think you can help me?
"I don't know either. We both agree it's not a matter of *solving* it. But how willing are we to *work* with it?"

I was thinking we agree it is not absolute, not either-or, even though there is a wish to be absolutely better or, at least, a lot better. But working with it might be a start, an opening. Will we, *can* we take it?

"What would working with it mean?" Gerry asked. "What would it be like?"

"It would be like working with each other," I offered. "And perhaps not just "like" but reaching for something more real."

I once asked a therapist of mine a similar question and she replied, "We can only try." In two years I did feel better, more than I thought I would. Even a little can make a big difference if it's real.

"We can try," Gerry said.

"We can only try," I nodded.

* * *

Gerry spoke of severe isolation. He once was engaged in life, significantly more than now, but since his last girlfriend left him two years earlier, he sank more and more into helpless paralysis. The last several months were an all-time low, nearly all his time spent in bed smoking. He imagined the room going up in flames, catching fire when a cigarette dropped out of his mouth while he slept.

> "I expected much more, so much more. Too bad you didn't know me when I was alive, maybe you'd stand a better chance of helping me. It must be impossible to imagine me as an alive person. I'd like just for an instant for you to have known me as I once was or could be sometimes—just so you'd know it's not impossible. How can you be motivated to work with this morass?"

"You're sure I can't see anything more?"

My mind came up with the words more-ass, which usually refers to getting laid. But the image that appeared was of someone vanishing up his own asshole. Disappearing, maybe hiding, then getting swallowed up. Jungians write about the "uroboros", a snake creating a circle, a hoop, its mouth holding its tail, eternity in time. I picture the snake swallowing itself two ways: swallowing itself tail and all and its tail swallowing it head and all. Two ways to disappeaar, bottom through mouth, top through ass. Freud associated anal functions with creativity. In the negative, it is associated with self-hate: "I'm a shit." No need to make a decision whether or how I or Gerry disappeared up our own or each other's asses. I cannot know for sure what having this set of images might mean. A powerful force in the room moving towards disappearance?

Gerry suddenly snapped into life, talking about a book he was writing before his girlfriend broke up the relationship. While I was dreaming about disappearing, a counter-movement began appearing.

"I was writing about creativity, how creativity makes you naked. A chapter on creativity anxiety. Creativity rips death apart. You have all these death shells, dead skin. You use your own death as protection.

"As I was writing I began saying thank you to the book. I listened, was it saying thank you to me too? The book was giving me myself. We were bringing each other into life, past protective shells. Can a book have a protective shell too? Its own death?

"In a flash the joke was on me. Death took over. Was I hoping to write death away or was death using me to write about life?

"Julia said she couldn't be with me anymore. She couldn't play my games. She said I wanted to dig my way into her, use her insides and she just wanted someone to be with. Is that when I died, turned to ice? I thought we were exploring our beings together. But I menaced her."

"What a shock," I felt. "To think you were writing about life and find you're writing about your death as it is happening or about to happen. You can't wish the death wish away—is that what creativity tries to do?

"How do you write?" I continued to muse, speaking almost as if to myself. "By grinding up the unconscious," came the answer. I thought of a rabbi who asked, "Why do we put salt on challah to welcome the Sabbath? Like salt, God adds invisible taste to everything." "Is that what we do when we write? Try to make God by grinding the salt?"

Gerry looked at me, astonished. "I don't know about tomorrow, but right now I found a partner," he said.

At that moment, I felt we shared something.

* * *

"I feel I'm bleeding."

"Where?"

"My heart, my stomach. In the hospital blood came out of my neck and I wondered if my head and body were attached. I couldn't tell if I was beheaded or be-bodied. Blood turned to tears, gushing down my arms. Blood and tears. Is there a difference? A blood knot.

"Notice I said I feel I'm bleeding. In the hospital I *was* bleeding or I could not tell if I was or wasn't. Now I can say I *felt* I was but then the feeling was real blood. Scary, isn't it?"

"The Bible says the soul is in the blood," I murmured.

"Scary to think feelings turn into blood. Feeling turns into blood and tears."

"Now you can see that. Now you know that. Many say in psychotherapy we put feeling into words. Does it sound right to say feelings turn into words? I always thought it a little funny, picturing words as bags you stuff feelings into."

"Words can be bloody," continued Gerry, adding, "And teary. Words can tear and be torn. Words can shred you."

"It's not true that sticks and stones can break your bones but words can never hurt you?" I gratuitously asked.

"Words can rip you to pieces," added Gerry. "A look or word can be devastating. A bad word tears your heart out."

I thought of times I was knocked out by someone's look or word. It is no accident that folklore speaks of an "evil eye". Or Judaism says that words create angels or demons when you speak. I picture myself writhing on the floor with a word sticking through my guts like a knife. Is there much of a difference between writhing and writing? I wonder, did I not start writing to express pain?

I remember a moment when a girl I was with gave me a bad look followed by hurtful words and minutes later I was sick. Not felt sick—*was* sick. Sickness spread through my chest and I was in bed for days. Years later, I saw the words "soul sickness" in William James and thought how sick the body can become at a point where difference between soul and body vanishes.

I was thinking how similar Gerry and I were, how feeling can become a concrete thing, blood, tears, illness.

> "I will sew myself up before the end of our session. I will put myself together before I leave, wipe the tears and blood. I will leave as if cleansed, as if pain is a kind of cleaner. I see bits of my soul in your face. You're feeling something too. Will the feelings dirty you or will they cleanse you too? Will you have to sew yourself up too?"
>
> "In a way, yes." I answered. "I sew myself too. But not altogether. Can't you feel we are permeable, we touch each other? That gives us something

we don't have to undo. We can let that simmer, take it away when we part."

Gerry holds his hands to his face, sobbing.

After some time in quiet, he says, "I so fear being without someone it is deadening. I can be with someone a few moments, not too long and it's OK, and then I want to get away. The air goes out of the room. Life leaves."

"Soul leaves, like blood," I add.

"Yes, it does not pay to be with someone. You can't breathe. Air is used up quickly."

We sit quietly until it is time to go. Gerry nods and says, "Thank you." "Thank you, too," I say. I thought of asking him say more, why did he thank me, but fortunately I held back and thought, "It's not easy being with another person so close and leaving alive, or more alive than when one came in. Gerry is so used to something bad happening and the bad is so used to dominating that it is baffled when there is room for the good."

* * *

"Room for the good." The words echoed as I left for the night. Was there room for the good? My skeptical mind wondered. An evil side of my heart guffawed. But a sliver of faith, a heart of faith nodded.

A woman once told me of a smile in the center of her heart, a heart smile that nothing could eclipse. I felt with her and wondered if some day I might feel that too.

* * *

"After last session I had a wonderful dream. I dreamt of a woman who gave me a good, long kiss. Or maybe it's closer to say we were kissing each other. What moved me was how long it was, no hurry. No rush to get it over and go to the next thing. So much of my life I felt rushed with no real reason to. In school maybe there was reason, having to keep up with the work one period to the next, day after day. But why would I think of being rushed in a kiss? What would I rush to? Rush to penetrate, to have intercourse, a rush to come? But no, not this time. This was a different kind of moment—no rush at all. Just the kiss itself. Nowhere else to go, nothing else to do. It was wondrous."

"Moments like that make you feel liked, good about being alive," I responded.

"Yes, exactly. I felt liked. She liked me. Kissing me wasn't a burden. She wanted to feel this too and she was in no rush either. I think I was learning from her. I didn't think of it then and maybe it's crazy—she was my teacher. Teaching me something about life, how not to rush, letting something good happen.

"Now I remember another dream that totally slipped away. On the left of the picture was the word "Establishment" and on the right the words "Artistic Spirit". That sums it up, a basic quandary. Creativity *vs.* Stultification."

"That is a basic choice, but does it have to be either-or?"

"I want to be more alive but am afraid to. It's easier being dead. I picture myself a corpse, embalmed. To be alive is hard work."

"What if the job has to do with creating yourself?"

"I don't think I can. I don't have the guts, the strength. I just don't have it. I'm too weak."

"Were you weak in the dream of the kiss?"

"I see what you're saying. It wasn't a matter of strong or weak. It was something that happened, a lucky moment."

"You didn't have to do anything except be there."

"It came after our session. Something good in the session became a good feeling in the dream."

I wanted to say, "You mean we were kissing each other?" I feared it would scare him. The kind of kiss I meant was inside, psyche to psyche.

"Something happened," he said. "Something went on between us."

"Something happened," I echoed. "It wasn't a matter of strong or weak. It was a matter of experiencing something happening."

A moment of experience, not forced, willed, intended. An unpredictable welling up. So often a welling up of bad things, but this time good.

"I'm afraid to tell you another dream fragment I had later, after getting up and going back to sleep. Almost its opposite. A tractor was chasing someone, some kind of pointy arrow or shovel chasing a woman? Not the one who kissed me—not her, I hope. Run away, run away, I yelled. I heard myself yelling as I woke. I'm afraid to think about this dream, I wish I didn't dream it.

"It's almost as if I have to dream something bad if I dream something good."

"I can think of so many reasons to run away, I hesitate to say."

"Are you afraid to be a therapist?"

"My thoughts seem so clichéd. You run to protect yourself. Something in you has to chase the woman away. You don't want to feel trapped, even by goodness. So much of your life you ran from threats. It's hard to know where the threat is coming from, who's threatening who or what. Goodness and danger, threats to each other."

"Cliché for you maybe, but for me a lot to think about. This sense of danger inside. One moment goodness, one moment danger. A sense of danger that doesn't go away even in the heart of goodness."

"And a sense of goodness that doesn't go away?" I ask.

"It keeps coming back," Gerry said.

We sit quietly.

After a while I find the following words forming: "Not too far, not too close, psyche to psyche with room to breathe." Wish or reality? Both?

* * *

"As I feared, after the reprieve, down the tubes," said Gerry. "I felt I found an oasis with you. But today goodness took a hit. Can it weather the attacks of Truth? Nothing is more dreadful. To be followed by Truth one knows one can't fulfill. The truth about oneself is menacing. What is left when truth comes? Nothing can withstand it."

"Everything seems a lie?" I answered.

"*Is* a lie, not seems. One has no recourse."

"Yes, we've touched a place known by many. Do you know the phrases of the past that say only God is good, man is chalked full of evil? Only God can save us."

"They knew what they were talking about. You go to this place and nothing in you can withstand the Critic."

I think of Holden Caulfield in *Catcher in the Rye* seeing the adult world as phony. Did Holden feel true? If so, what kind of free pass did he have for himself, how did he get it? Or is there always good and evil and it gets split up, divided in different ways? This part of me is good, this part of me is bad. This section of humanity is good, this section of humanity is bad. Jesus and the hypocrites, Jesus the true, hypocrites the false. Can it be so easy? I am beginning to feel more on Gerry's side. His plight seems true to me in some way: the truth that nothing can withstand the truth.

I feel like throwing myself on my knees and praying and picture Gerry and I begging for mercy. There is nothing we can do to save ourselves. Saint Paul must have seen something like this when he said the good law is unfulfillable. Can you find a mustard seed of Faith and Grace, can it find you?

"In the hospital I cried out, 'Save me, save me!' The cries wrenched my heart. Can one save oneself? I don't see how. All the piss and shit and bugs inside. The psychiatrist in the hospital said to imagine a detox system, a sewer system inside. That helped a little, drained a little. But it's the self, *me* that's poisoned and poisonous. You tried to teach me that so much of this is self-hate. Hate turned against the self. But it's deeper, the self itself is toxic."

"So we've gotten back to original sin," I say. "The human race has felt it a very long time, tried to counteract it so many ways." I think of Fairbairn saying that depressives feel their hate is bad and schizophrenics feel their love is bad.

I feel as helpless as Gerry in face of our nature but have some modicum of good feeling I cannot kill, good that stands up to me, stands on its own. A gift, a grace, a part of what I was born into. A thread that lifts life.

"I'm touched by your face," says Gerry. "I feel you are touched by me. Something is there, a tone. I can attack it but I see you are devoted to being here with me."

What I was silently going through must have translated into devotional feeling that Gerry sensed. A feeling of crying from our hearts touched Gerry's sensors without words.

"You don't have to be in a hospital for your heart to cry" I said, moved that he felt my feeling.

I began to think we were going to end up in a better place than I feared. It looked as if we were plunging down with no way out. Unexpected, unplanned, a reprieve began by staying with the plunge. Staying with no way out is a way out. Something opens in no-opening.

"An oasis is coming back," says Gerry.

* * *

After the session and for the rest of the day, a simple image kept appearing, sun after storm. So clichéd that it is part of Disney films, animals hiding in the forest until the rain stops and sun comes out. Such a simple fit between the outside and inside world. Darkness comes, sunlight comes. Movement of one feeling to another. Even Freud in his letters to Fliess used the terms darkness–light to express creative processes. Basic, simple, real.

* * *

"I feel I survived an attack of cruel truth, although I don't know what the truth is—unless it's simply how bad I am," began Gerry. "I think that's it. That I survived feeling how bad I am."

"Accepting that I'm a hopeless case has been very freeing," I respond.

"I've heard it said that one good moment is enough in the court of heaven."

"I suspect that for some whose point of goodness can't escape the black hole, none is enough."

We sat in peace for a time.

Stirrings began.

"I was moved to tears by a woman I saw last night. We passed each other by but our faces linked like train cars coupling yet delicately. My heart filled with tears."

"Because you passed each other, missed each other—uncoupling?" I suggested.

"Something deeper. Her face moved my soul. I'm not sure why. I can make up words but that's not it."

"A soul of depths," I said.

"That's closer," said Gerry. "Not quite, but closer."

After a few more minutes he tried again.

"It's like seeing all life as a moment," he started. "You feel all the grief and beauty rolled up in one face, a glance. In the movies, you can sink into someone's face. I felt my soul sink into hers. And then she was gone, except for the feeling, rippling, fading, like time. Time itself touched and left me, as it often does, but this time quintessentially.

"Last night I had another dream of a woman kissing me. A long, accepting kiss. My chest relaxed. I'm beginning to catch on. Cruel attacks and warmth. When I'm in the first, I feel only the bad is real. When I'm in the second, I feel I've gotten a moment's reprieve. I know the bad thing is coming back. Any moment, shorter, longer, a certainty. What's less certain is the good moment. Yet, it does come back and in new ways and I'm very relieved and grateful for the relief."

"A basic rhythm?"

"A rhythm I can't count on. I can count on the bad coming after good but am afraid the good will never return, as if devastated forever."

"I shouldn't say this. Forgive me. But I can't help thinking you're in good company. The end of the books of Moses poses a question as to whether good or evil will win. And near the end of Freud's works, he wonders whether the life drive will win over the death drive or not."

"Maybe he felt more life than I. But I can't say I'm without it. That's the learning here. Even I can't admit I'm without it.

"This may not sound like much, but a girl I was with felt a need to warn me about her tricks. She said she fuses with others to make them think she likes them. To make them think she's one with them. She uses a sense of being one with others to disarm them. I thought that was a way of protecting herself and said I guess that was a way of making herself feel less a threat—and less threatening. You have to pretend not to be you for God–mom to love you? She quieted down and started listening to me and, to my surprise, I began to feel we were both mysteries. Mystery itself. I was afraid feeling that would scare me—fear of breakdown. Instead, I felt free."

"You don't have be tied to being you?"

"Mystery is freeing."

* * *

I think what happened was that Gerry tapped a moment beyond good and bad that felt good. In that moment, disputes dropped away. A surge of mystery took him past anxiety. Hints of another sense of being.

* * *

"I'm thinking about the thing that doesn't go away."

"The bad thing or the good thing?" I asked.

"I was going to say the bad thing but now I don't know. An image of Jesus dying and coming to life comes and I think that is the way life feels. Death–life together. Agony dying into joy, elements in life's feeling.

"I want to tell you that when I was at my worst in the hospital it was also my best. I felt something more than I ever did. It terrified me but . . . Now I think it was the terror that filled me, that made me feel something more. Terror more than I am. Now I am less than I am.

"When I was in the hospital my worst states opened a door, a glimpse of what can never be grasped. Realities I scarcely have inklings of, that go on beyond me, without me. For a moment a door opened."

"And now you long for it . . ."

"With all my being . . . no, not true. Can something be true and not true? With all my being—true. Yet glad I'm less and can walk around in my life outside the hospital. Do you know what it's like to be confined? You come out and feel free. You can breathe. Would you say that must be one of the greatest gifts—to leave the womb and breathe on your own?"

"More than yourself, less than yourself," I echo.

"Who can measure?"

"Pascal called us a disproportion," I add.

"A disproportion that is more and less than itself, " Gerry corrects me.

"Do you know, I find it beautiful to listen to you?" I say. "I feel you have a real sense of beauty."

"Thank you. Right now I feel like what we are doing is helping me find my nose. Are we doing psychoanalysis? A psychoanalytic nose after all kinds of elusive scents. My definition of freedom: from clogged nose to a nose that breathes and smells.

"There is a hole in my heart. When I try to find what's in it I vanish. I haven't gotten the knack of being in and out at the same time. I get the idea that the thing that blows me up links me together. Someone close to me warned me I would drown in my own feelings. Try to stay above the ocean of emotions. When I am falling asleep I feel deep peace. Sometimes, I weep and feel whatever is wrong with me takes me deeper. I think what makes me weep is being moved by my life."

"That makes me weep too, being moved by life, my life, our lives," I share.

"We are on top of a mountain and the mountain is on top of us. I don't pretend to know what that means. But it is what I feel."

CHAPTER TWELVE

Affect images and states

Years ago, I attended a New School lecture by Henry Elkin, who said, "Beneath every neurosis is a hidden psychosis." Along this line he later added, "If you want proof of the Jungian archetypes, just go crazy." Elkin was an anthropologist who, after a psychotic episode, found his deeper vocation as a depth psychologist. He trained in Zurich with Emma Jung and continued growing the rest of his life. Loray Daws (2016) recently brought together Elkin's papers, which express aspects of his profound exploration of the human condition.

In *The Psychotic Core* (2004a), I wrote about affect worlds buried in Freud's abstract formulations. His depiction of psychic structures and processes contains an implicit phenomenology of psychotic states as well as more general affective life. In this chapter, I will pull a few affect words out of the hat and follow some lines of movement.

Freud (Bonaparte & Kris, 1954) wrote of "flooding" as a primal trauma. He seems to conjoin outer–inner stimuli flooding, including drives, with emotional flooding. I picture the biblical God's disappointment and rage at human failure producing an emotional flood wiping out existence. Perhaps like a baby screaming to blot out pain.

Bion (1994) related feelings of empty–full to the early feeding situation as a kind of model for a sense of emotional emptiness–fullness. He also spoke of a psychotic big bang in which bits and pieces of the psyche sped away from the point of origin (O) and each other at increasing velocity. Complex relations between what may be experienced as creative–destructive aspects of O can vex, damage, and uplift (Bion, 1970; Eigen, 1998).

What materials we are given to work with throughout our lives! We note a double sense of chaos–nothingness, too much–too little, emptiness–plenitude. Bion depicts a maddening state of maximum–minimum emotion, oscillating and simultaneous. Animals share some of this, although our magnifying–minifying psyche may take it to further dimensions, imaginative, mythic, poetic, white and horrific lies. In graduate school, we learned of experiments with rats in which too much or too little arousal could lead to paralysis on the one hand and inertia on the other. When not put out of play by too much or too little, rats became curious about the environment and explored. Paralysis–inertia, states we not only share with fellow creatures but also imaginatively elaborate.

Freud balanced his concern with flooding with depictions of psychic depletion. He contrasted highly vital states with loss of energy, desire, and movement. Before Freud's theory of active libido taking many forms, Pierre Janet, working with hospitalized individuals, related mental breakdowns to psychic weakness in the sense that psyche was unable to hold it all together and began to disintegrate under pressure. Related to this, the notion of "ego strength" was later used to predict better or worse outcomes for those undergoing psychotic states. Another term used was capacity of "executive functions" in organizing experience. Some seem to have more capacity to function while undergoing states that could derail others. There are many experiential spectrums and outcomes.

While Winnicott (1992) tends to emphasize environmental trauma, Bion also speaks to a deficit in human capacity to tolerate its own states. We produce states we do not have equipment to handle or work with well. A Bion emphasis is difficulty tolerating the build-up of affective intensity and ways we not only try to tone it down but get rid of it ("evacuation"). We can blow up with too much and become affect deprived with too little.

I do not intend to oppose Winnicott and Bion here. Winnicott, too, writes of the challenge of developing capacity to sustain experiencing. For example, he writes of primitive agonies in infancy before we have capacity to process them, which, especially when reinforced by trauma, can leave us with lifelong fear of beginnings. In essence, we learn from psychoanalysis that being alive and being a psychical being is itself traumatic, which environmental experiences can extend, overplay, and underplay. The incapacity addressed by Winnicott and Bion is one we work with throughout life (Eigen, 2004d).

We are born and aborted all life long. Lacan (1981) speaks of difficulties being psychically born. Being born entails experiencing lack. Lacan includes loss of the placenta. To be born means to leave something behind, in some way give up something. And to be born entails experiencing mortality. One day life and being will be left behind, one will die. I think of an example Elkin spoke about in class about a visit to a hospital where one of the patients seemed to be in the predicament of being unable to decide "whether to remain an immortal god or become a human being." A double sense of immortality–mortality seems part of human experience and has been so since pre-antiquity, each state often played against and/or fused with the other.

Some individuals describe not leaving the placenta behind. For example, Sergei Pankejeff, "The Wolf Man," depicts a caul, a veil around his experience, so that life cannot become fully alive or fully lived (Freud, 1918b; Teitelbaum, 2016). It is a state described by many modern authors, for example, Camus's *The Stranger* or Gide's *The Immoralist*. When Samuel Beckett's therapy with Bion was over, Bion took him to a lecture by Jung as a kind of celebration to mark the moment. It turned out to be an extremely meaningful evening for Beckett. Jung spoke of a woman who did not feel born or who, Jung might say, was not, or failed to be, born. Beckett, in a moment of recognition, said, "That's me." You can feel in his work a lifelong struggle with this issue, to which he gives expression over and over.

Language can null and create experience. When we speak of "putting feeling into words" it often is at the expense of loss of feeling. But it can also, at times, create new feeling, as Rilke does as he writes. Bion (1984) comments on this at the end of his collection of early essays, *Second Thoughts*. The essays, written near the beginning of Bion's practice, focused on psychotic processes. In one of his autobiographical remarks, he wryly states he wrote them to get referrals.

But they are striking probes of the human condition. I do not know if there was anything he said or wrote that did not light up the psyche.

In *Second Thoughts*, he added a lengthy look back at these earlier papers and noted how some of the things he said to a patient furthered experiencing and some cut it off. For example, he recounted his remarks to dreams the patient shared, and showed which furthered or blocked the dreaming experience. Remarks that seemed in sync with the dream feeling, a kind of intuitive immersion, opened further flow, whereas "talking about" hindered it. There is a significant difference between talking *from* a feeling or talking *about* it, letting a feeling talk or shutting it down with premature presumptive knowledge.

Bettelheim (1972) and Arieti (1974) both wondered if loss of intensity is a function of getting better. Both write of overwhelming states in the height of psychotic episodes that wane, with mourning for loss of intensity. Can the intensity revealed in psychotic moments add to life in general? Along this line, Winnicott (1992) remarked that he was sane most of his life and as he grew older felt more aliveness dipping into moments of madness he now could access. In *Psychic Deadness* (2004c), I bring out spectrums of aliveness–deadness that are part of living, including combinations and extremes in both directions. Partnering our capacities is an evolutionary challenge rather than a matter of final solution.

A man who went through multiple hospitalizations and has been hospital free for the ten years we have been working went through a period of sleeping in gutters. I felt afraid for him, what was he exposing himself to, would he survive the dangers of the city, infection? Was I being irresponsible not sending him to the emergency room? Yet, he said his ability to do this was keeping him out of hospital.

His look compelled me, desperate, longing, and his words felt as if he was letting out something toxic that poisoned him. He said as much. "The gutter is where I belong. The sewer is underneath. I can feel it, smell it. I would sleep in the sewer but the gutter somehow links below, surface, above. I don't want to be trapped below. I need to show this awful thing. I want people to see it."

Many times he told me he is made of shit. The sewer is where he belongs. But he has gotten to a point where he wants to show what is in him. He wants people to know how he smells. In the sewer, one could not tell the difference between his smell and its smell.

Language associates self-hate with fecal images. You're shit, I'm shit. Animals smell and lick fecal matter, a fecal *savoir*. We smell and lick each other's psyches and our own. "I want you to see my no-goodness, rottenness. I want you to smell me." The Bible speaks of knowing the other through sexuality. But we know each other through all our senses. How does one feel oneself? Proprioception, kinesthesia? What is it one feels when one feels oneself? I think my patient is trying to feel himself. When I suggested this to him he said, "Lying in the gutter feels real. It's where I belong. Danger adds to it. Maybe someone will take me by surprise, kill me, rape me. I feel I'm crying now thinking of it. I'm crying inside."

> *Mike*: Crying is real.
> *Don*: I could put it down. Alligator tears? Eaten by tears inside. Torn to pieces. I have moments of peace in the gutter, moments of peace in the danger. It's where I belong.
> *Mike*: "All the time?"
> *Don*: I love to walk. Maybe that's my favorite thing. Walking anywhere. Going and going. In some way I feel like trains I watched as a kid. Nothing could stop them. Then I heard of derailing and people getting crushed. If you're made of steel movement can be dangerous. I'm just a person and get skinned by falling. What do you think of tripping on your own feet?
> *Mike*: Like biting your tongue or cheek?
> *Don*: Pain you cause yourself.
> *Mike*: There's a lot of it.
> *Don*: You've touched that point again, that spot, a pain spot with a well filled with tears.
> *Mike*: Can you find it? For me it's about here. [I point to the middle of my chest, our treasure chest.]
> *Don*: Yes, I feel it there too now.
> *Mike*: It's very beautiful.
> *Don*: "How can that be?"

Not too long after this conversation, Don began sleeping in Riverside Park where he heard the Hudson River and boats, saw the starlight and was permeated by the scent of grass. In retrospect, I began thinking he needed to integrate the fecal self, or at least acknowledge it and have it acknowledged. The fecal self we all share. To show and share self-denigration, self-hatred, or, as Freud might write, "aggression against oneself." An appetite for self-debasement opened to an appetite for something more, in this case beginnings of a deeper soul beauty. Don and I have come a long way and are still together through many changes. He spends a lot of time painting and more recently has become intrigued by sculpting, shares an apartment, and feels new longings.

CHAPTER THIRTEEN

Everything human; hidden sprouts and psyche talk*

To graduate from a psychoanalytic institute is no small thing, considering the hardships and challenges one goes through. Training in many other professions is hard enough, but in psychoanalysis one's very person is at stake, one's most intimate psyche at risk. If you have teachers in law or medical school that are not *simpatico*, you might have a rough time, but you work hard and get through. In psychoanalysis, when you have misalignment between student and teacher, one's very existence is in danger of misinterpretation. If you hide, you will be seen as hiding. If you show yourself, you are open to misunderstanding. Your very being, who you are as a person, is on the line.

The fact that you are here this evening means you have weathered such experiences and weathered them well. It also means that it is likely that you found links you value, that helped enrich your relation to emotional reality, and that all your positive and negative

---

* "Everything human," Graduation talk, The National Psychological Association for Psychoanalysis (NPAP), September 24, 2010.
"Hidden sprouts and psyche talk." New York University Postdoctoral Program in Psychotherapy and Psychoanalysis, June 8, 2007.

experiences together helped you find ways to mediate the emotional reality of others.

With all the difficulties of our time, this is one of the richest moments to be a psychoanalyst. Psychoanalysis interfaces a broad range of disciplines and influences—spirituality, cultural studies, infant research, neurology, to name but a few. Bion felt psychoanalysis is still very much an unknown baby, even embryonic. What psychoanalysis is and can be is a work in progress. As so much in life, one learns about it by doing it. And as one does it and does it more and more, one senses that whatever this strange beast is, this baby, it has special contributions to make. No other field quite covers the ground psychoanalysis does. It is a new thing in human relations, in human experience, two people together probing depths and nuances of experience in the ways we do, sometimes breaking new ground in what it is possible to experience. In this, it makes a special contribution to cultural history and, to my thinking, psychic evolution.

Time is short, so I will jump into some of what I want to say, which means leaving a lot out. This, I fear, is the state of things in many moments of life. Which makes what we are able to say all the more vulnerable and sometimes, with luck, valuable. Our situation reminds me of jumping from stone to stone crossing a brook when I was a child. Such a thrill, jump, jump! And, lo!, we alight on the other side. What is it Dogen says? "Words are bits and pieces leaping out."

So much of what we work with is invisible, ineffable. You may be able to measure galvanic skin reflexes or chemicals or brain images associated with anxiety—but anxiety itself? You can feel it, but can you touch or see it? You create images to express it. You sense it with a special psychic sense. A sense that senses feelings. Some people feel it in or through their skin. Others in their gut or heart or throat or rectum. For others, it's all over, nowhere, in the air, gripping them in unknown ways from invisible insides. Insides that cannot be found anywhere.

Freud spoke of a sense organ for the perception of psychical qualities that must be studied for its own sake. And the only way it can be studied is by being used. You have to use it to know it. You have to build this mysterious capacity, the capacity to sense emotional qualities. In some ways, animals have it. They sense danger or food or a possible mate. With us, the matter is even more complex. Dogs may sniff assholes to get a sense of another dog. We sniff psyches. We have in us a special sense organ that sniffs, tastes, "gets the feel" of another human being, and gets the feel of one's own life. How does one's own life feel? It is a question one never stops asking.

Freud called consciousness an organ for sensing psychical qualities. It is likely that pre-conscious and unconscious processes play a role in this sensing, too. We are not going to solve all the issues clustering around our psychic sensing capacity today, perhaps ever. But we are pointing to something important to us, however we understand it, whatever we do with it or it with us.

There was once a time when a person in the midst of psychotic breakdown might speak of soul murder and the doctor or helper or witness would not have a clue. There are not many of you today who could not relate to someone speaking of soul murder, whatever it might turn out to mean. The idea of soul murder is familiar to you. You have a feel for it. The psychic sensing of some portion of humanity has grown to encompass it or, at least, make contact with possible realities it touches. Schreber and history have taught us, at least alerted us, to realities that must be worked with, whether or not we can.

When I began practice, what soon came to be called "borderlines" exploded on the scene. What to do with such raw sensitivity, reactivity, sensitive anger, sensitive wounds. You could be in the middle of what seemed like a productive conversation about important concerns, when, without warning, a hole in the earth opened and you dropped into it, a hole your patient told you about but now you knew first hand. Another apple, another bite. Holes in the universe, verbal–emotional land mines, opening everywhere.

For years, the literature was filled with issues about borderline anger. At some point, it dawned on me that a function of that anger was to peck the response system needed by the patient into being. A growth in psychic sensing was needed. Now, many therapists feel at home with so-called "borderlines." Not that it is easy, but they tend to "know", that is, "sense", what to do because the response system to work with this level of wounded, angry sensitivity has begun to develop. A spontaneous, long-term growth of psychic sensing and know-how was called into being by stubborn reaction to injury.

At this moment of history, something similar has to happen with problems related to psychopathy. The term "psychopathy" is not used anymore. It has been changed to "sociopathy," which has merits. Maybe both terms should be used, pointing to social and psychical aspects of loss of feeling for others in the process of trying to get what one thinks one wants. Many years ago we were taught that psychopathy had to do with defective conscience. I would emphasize lack of sensitive caring about the feelings of others one injures. In our success-oriented world, getting ahead is more important than worrying about what happens to others as one moves along. One's own success and survival is what counts. This attitude, a kind of psychopathy of everyday life, is endemic in individuals and the larger social scene.

An egregious example is our pre-emptive bombing of Iraq, lest it destroy or damage us with its (nonexistent) nuclear capability. Whether the reason was power, position, prestige, oil—our leaders psychopathically manipulated psychotic anxieties to exploit minds and have its way. A sense of the harm caused to real living people seemed less important than position, money, and power. They milked and displaced fear of terrorism to pursue what they imagined was a king of the hill policy. Lying to get one's way is part of the fabric of public discourse.

When I was younger, I was taught that you cannot analyze a liar. Analysis was about truth and analyst and patient alike were in pursuit of it. That may be so. But lying is also ubiquitous, part of how consciousness works. And if you cannot analyze a liar, you cannot analyze anyone. Especially since a liar is also doing the analyzing. This is a challenge that exercises us today.

The resilience and resistance and well nigh universality of psychopathic tendencies is knocking on our door, knocking on our psyches and, one hopes, in time will stimulate response systems to meet it. Is psychic sensing enabling work with psychopathy growing in the wings? Can we sense it, help mediate it, grow with it? It will not mean we will become lie-free beings. We can no more stop lying than breathing. But there may be ways we can learn to sense and work with our amazing lying resourcefulness in less destructive ways.

Can we open a larger, more productive space where lying and truthing dance and play? Truth is not simply a casualty. Truth often is used destructively and the damage is downplayed. It may be more important to be a kindly liar or truth teller rather than one who uses either capacity to dominate, degrade, and kill. Affective attitude plays a role in how capacities are used. It may be no accident that we are in an Age of Psychopathy *and* an Age of Sensitivity.

I suspect the sense of being right has caused as much or more damage in human history than any other attitude. I have never met a psychopath who did not think he was right. It is as if he has a right to get what he wants and redress injury by scoring over others. Robert Fliess, son of Wilhelm, pointed out long ago that self-righteousness is part of the attitude of child abusers. In *The Psychotic Core*, I worried that Russia or the United States, during the cold war, would miscalculate from the viewpoint of omniscience, thinking they knew something they did not, and push the nuclear button. The situation is more fragmented and complex, but no less fragile now.

Miscalculation from omniscience, thinking one knows more than one does, thinking one is right, psychopathic manipulation of psychotic anxieties—When Jesus said, "Forgive them, Father, they don't know what they're doing," he hit the nail on the head. Our psychopathic tendency always knows or makes believe it knows. Not knowing . . . waiting . . . is this part of the sensing we are growing into, need more of?

To be able to feel and say, "I don't know"—a freeing moment? a gateway to the psychoanalytic attitude? Jesus linked not knowing with compassion. I think in psychoanalysis we can also link it with opening, the radical opening of the psychoanalytic attitude.

Rumi has passages in which he supports an attitude that welcomes all guests. Rumi makes room. He means inner guests as well as outer. The insides of others, of oneself. The play of inner–outer often mystifies, invites, challenges. Our moment-to-moment work is variable, depending on fatigue, time of day, attitude, how our children are doing, how our own life feels, and so many more factors. But in the slowing down of time that often happens in sessions, we have another moment, and another. And another day, or week, or month. Part of a therapy couple's learning is coming through variability, moment after moment, day after day, coming through so many changes in quality.

Time can fool one; it has so many forms. A patient recently thought of leaving after twenty-five years. "Twenty-five years," she said. And we sat with the feeling. How did they pass so quickly? They seemed to go on and on forever. Sessions are often like that. Time slows down during the session. We drop into forever details or possibilities. And then the session ends. Where did time go? I wonder if any of you feel like that about institute training time?

Bion writes, "The fundamental reality is 'infinity', the unknown, the situation for which there is no language – not even one borrowed by the artist or the religious – which gets anywhere near to describing it" (1994, p. 372). "Psychoanalysis itself is just a stripe on the coat of the tiger. Ultimately it may meet the Tiger – The Thing Itself – O" (Bion, 1990, p. 112).

You are that stripe, that Tiger, that Reality. There is no end to what you will meet, no end to this limitless introduction to yourselves and your patients. Bion said psychoanalysis helps introduce the patient to him/herself. Part of what makes this possible is the atmosphere of the analyst's own self-introduction that never stops. We are such intricate, challenging creatures, so alone, so interweaving. I like what a little tweak of a word can do: alone: all-one. With a blink of the eye, alone. With a blink of the eye: all-one.

The Bion quotes about no language exhausting the sensed impact of infinite reality—indeed, language itself becomes part of this impact—is a reminder that the psyche is more unknown than known. If we think we know only a little about a small portion of the matter of the universe, how much less do we know about psychical reality? Bear this in mind when you get drawn into wars between "schools" and disciplines, with all their contributions and limitations. Paradoxically, realization of such immensity can be freeing as well as paralyzing. If you do not think that what you do is the all of everything, you may be freer to give your all to it.

From my earliest days in the field, I felt a sense of practicing at the margins and a sense that psychoanalysis was a marginal formation in our economic age. Yet, I felt at the center of things, that I was contributing from the inside. Psychoanalysis brought me close to the center of life, my life, my attempts to live life. It permeated me and gave me tools to struggle, more, it grew and changed with me, as if we were both babies learning to live, learning to live together, a daily creative process.

Some analysts, some people in the arts, convert their disciplines into impressive financial profit. Many do not—poets rarely do, then there is the proverbial actor as waiter. I am not suggesting you all go out and become waiters. You do enough waiting in the service we are in. But I wish to support you in freeing the value of your practice from how much it makes. I never felt that money was the all-encompassing measure of value. Today in our offices and next week too, we may do something, feel or say or think something with another person, that will over time make a difference in life lived.

Often growth happens when you are not looking. Bion called faith the psychoanalytic attitude, psychoanalytic faith, including openness to what is unknown in a session, unknown realities that exert transforming impacts.

Much that happens opens reality, if we can find ways to work with it.

Hidden sprouts and psyche talk

When I first heard psychoanalysis was dead or dying. I was confused because psychoanalysis was—and is—so alive for me. How could something so alive for me be so dead for others, many others, the greater culture? As dead as god or, at least, on the way to being a dead god. Yet wherever I look I find traces of psychoanalytic-like ideas and images and thought forms. Does this mean the remains of psychoanalysis are embedded in thought and language and imagery like fossils? Or does psychoanalysis have a secret life masked by official narratives?

Yale University is now beginning a psychoanalytic studies program, a sub-specialty of the Department of Literature. The link between psychoanalysis and literature is fitting, given that the only official prize Freud's work won in his lifetime was the Goethe prize for literature. In his early work on hysteria, Freud commented that phrases such as "stab in the heart" or "blow to the face" are not mere figures of speech. They are accurate portrayals of how psychic injury feels.

Psychoanalysis and literature share a dedicated concern with meaning and how life feels and is lived. Who are we? What are we doing? What sorts of capacities do we have? How are we constituted? What *is* this life we are living? I suspect the link between psychoanalysis and literature at Yale will be mutually nourishing.

Much "official" talk today is about psychoanalysis and science, brain imagery, chemistry. Yet, psychoanalysis also thrives in the interstices of meaning and experience and a hunger for wild thoughts. Over twenty years ago, in *The Psychotic Core*, I wondered if the unconscious was on its way to being outlawed.

Literature is not yet outlawed, although corporate marketing cuts off areas of its flow. I would not be surprised if the depths and guts and heart of writing and psychoanalysis vanish into underground streams, secretly keeping an important part of life alive. Such a vanishing, of course, is replenishing. There is a hunger for psyche-talk that commodification (commode) of science and marketing sound bites cannot satisfy.

I once wondered about, but am no longer surprised by, the number of psychiatrists who find their way into my talk and listen and sense and feel office. In their practice, medication rules. But they are looking for something else or more in their lives. I am not suggesting dialogue and medication are mutually exclusive, but that soul talk is essential. There are modes of nourishment that support our existence as persons and we are barely able to perceive them. The big picture dwarfs smaller differences. Virtually all sorts of psychoanalytic schools offer some sort of psyche-talk.

Ways of doing psyche-talk change, including the range and selection of what can be talked about. Freud once wrote to Fliess that psychoanalysis was akin to ancient mystery cults. Both were involved in psychic transformations. It is not surprising that the medium of transformation is itself transformed by what it undergoes and we are very much engaged in such a process.

If someone like Schreber—possibly diagnosed as having bipolar paranoid psychosis—walked into our office and spoke about soul-murder today, few people in this room would blink twice. We would take it in our stride and ask Judge Schreber to tell us more about his soul-murder, tell us everything, anything. We would empathize with his tale of injury. We would listen and respond and over time our capacity to respond to his particular soul-murder would develop. Our sensibility and attunement is not the same as it might have been had we practiced when Freud wrote his great account of this sensitive man who gave us so much.

In the past forty years, I have witnessed the growth of another psychic area, our response to "borderline psychotic individuals". I remember how thrown we were by our first borderlines so many decades ago. The capacity to treat them had not yet arrived.

The combination of supersensitivity and rage grabbed and challenged me. I felt I was being let in on an area of being in which pain and agony were infinitely magnified, psyche a torture chamber. One moment you thought the individual was on the way to a hospital, the next the storm subsided, another soon on the way. In a few years came a period where individuals who failed with another therapist would come in and rail against the whole therapy field with its insidious promise and uselessness. Being with a borderline in those days felt like being thrown off a bronco over and over and being kicked in the gut over and over. To feel like a failure seemed to be part of my vocation.

Eventually, I thought of a bird we studied in physiological psychology. I do not remember its name, but in this mother–baby couple, the baby had to peck the mother in a specific spot in the neck for her mothering response to kick into gear. The baby needed to peck the mothering response into being. This I felt the borderline doing with her super sensitivity and rage. She pecked at our response capacity, trying to peck into being the right combination of psychic nutrients. In time, the pecking succeeded. Now, forty years later, many of us automatically, naturally, spontaneously have the response equipment needed to help the so-called borderline.

So now that we do have the response capacity borderlines need (at least some of us, certainly most in this room!)—where is the edge of the possible? One edge is psychopathy. We are living through a time of psychopathy raised to new levels of insensitivity. Leaders of our country do not seem to care about injury they inflict as long as they are dominant. Our government serves corporate profit and power at enormous psychic and environmental cost. It is an attitude that trickles down from the top, reinforcing a sense that strength is getting away with things as long as you win and weakness is to be a sucker and lose. Having feelings is for sissies. Exploitation is for winners.

A few decades ago, in *The Psychotic Core*, I described a pervasive structure of madness in our times characterized by a megalomanic mental ego dissociatively linked with a fusional–explosive body ego. That structure still holds. But today the problem is somewhat different or has a different emphasis. We live in an Age of Psychopathy, in which triumphal psychopathic manipulation of psychotic agonies hold masses of people in thrall.

At this juncture of history, it is crucial for all of society to grow the response capacity needed to address our psychopathy. We must do this on smaller and larger scales and anything any of us can do on any front, whether in our office, our home, our own minds, or in the larger world, is to the good. Every little bit counts. To build response capacity needed to work with psychopathy is a pressing evolutionary edge. The quality of our physical *and* psychic world depends on it. Perhaps the destruction psychopathy brings will "peck" a capacity to work with it into being—a fearful, sorely needed awakening that sufficient horror might evoke.

When I was a young analyst it used to be thought that you cannot analyze a liar and you cannot analyze a psychopath. Our picture of truth and lies is more complex now. W. R. Bion was on to this some time ago, when he noted that lying is ubiquitous. With our current knowledge one can say, if you cannot analyze a liar, you cannot analyze anyone, since a liar also does the analyzing. No one is exempt from psychopathy in everyday life. But when this tendency threatens the very conditions that support life, we must learn to work with it.

You never know how help will come. I was jogging in the park and a bright red soccer shirt caught my eye. It had the word "Essien" on it. I wondered what Essien was? A business that sponsored a team? Was it connected with something mystical, the ancient Essenes sect, which my mind connects with the Yiddish "essen", to eat, to nourish. Mystical nourishment? Related to es, esse, is, to be? I spoke to the young man who wore the shirt. His look hardened and he glared at me. Maybe he thought I was hitting on him or maybe he just did not like old white guys. He scared me and maybe I scared him. It was quick, fleeting. When I asked if Essien was a business, he smiled. When I asked if it was his name, he shook his head in disbelief. "A player?" I ventured. "A great one," he whispered. "You should watch him sometime."

"I used to watch games when my kids were young," I said. "Now they're grown and away from home like dispersed seeds." We looked at each other, smiling in our particular ways. I saw the youngness, the angles of his face clearly. The hard angles that frightened me before now warmed me. A tough mistrust that crusted each of us thawed. "Take care," he called as I continued to jog by. "Take care too," I echoed.

I felt we were planting seeds in each other, that he was planted in me and I in him. Can such a moment bear fruit? It already has. I believe in moments.

In sessions we are often like deer stranded in the middle of the road, staring into headlights of the mind. Life has shifted around us.

Instead of a forest, we are frozen in fast traffic. Nothing stops. Sessions fly too fast for our mindsets. But there are some sessions that wait for us, let us catch up to them, and we swim along together for a while. That might make us think we are good at something, but more deeply we are moved by the immensity we work with and care about.

I think of unfillable fathomlessness of Lao Tzu and hidden sprouts unrushed to ripen. An uncarved block form does not exhaust, like Michelangelo's slaves ever emerging from inexhaustible backgrounds. Once, speaking about these things, a woman said, "But that's impossible." "Yes, impossible," I said, "but you feel something." "Something precious," she said.

Gradual sounds related to graduation, gradually beginning, ripening, steeping. To steep in new ways of being together, a beautiful journey, few thrills greater than the living psyche.

REFERENCES

Arieti, S. (1974). *Interpretation of Schizophrenia*. New York: Basic Books.
Berdyaev, N. (1975). *Slavery and Freedom*, R. M. French (Trans.). New York: Charles Scribner's Sons.
Bergson, H. (1911). *Creative Evolution*, A. Mitchell (Trans.). New York: Henry Holt.
Bettelheim, B. (1972). *The Empty Fortress: Infantile Autism and the Birth of the Self*. New York: Free Press.
Bion, F. (1995). The days of our lives. *Journal of Melanie Klein and Object Relations*, 13(1). Available at: www.psychoanalysis.org.uk/days.htm
Bion, W. R. (1970). *Attention and Interpretation*. London: Tavistock.
Bion, W. R. (1984). *Second Thoughts: Selected Papers on Psychoanalysis*. London: Karnac.
Bion, W. R. (1987). Making the best of a bad job. *Clinical Seminars and Four Papers*. London: Karnac.
Bion, W. R. (1990). *A Memoir of the Future*. London: Karnac.
Bion, W. R. (1994). *Cogitations*, F. Bion (Ed.). London: Karnac.
Bonaparte, M., & Kris, E. (Eds.) (1954). *The Origins of Psychoanalysis: Sigmund Freud's Letters, Drafts and Notes to Wilhelm Fliess (1887–1902)*, E. Mosbacher & J. Strachey (Trans.). London: Image.
Chuang Tzu (1964). *Chuang Tzu: Basic Writings*, B. Watson (Trans.). New York: Columbia University Press.

Cleckley, H. M. (1941). *The Mask of Sanity*. Uploaded by Emily S. Cleckley, 1988: www.cix.co.uk/~klockstone/sanity_1.pdf

Daws, L. (Ed.) (2016). *On the Origin of the Self: The Collected Papers of Henry Elkin, PhD*. Missoula, MO: EPIS Press.

Eddington, A. S. (1929). *The Nature of the Physical World*. New York: Macmillan.

Eigen, M. (1981) The area of faith in Winnicott, Lacan and Bion. *International Journal of Psychoanalysis, 62*: 413-433 [reprinted in: *The Electrified Tightrope*, London: Karnac, 2004a].

Eigen, M. (1992). *Coming Through the Whirlwind*. Wilmette, IL: Chiron.

Eigen, M. (1998). *The Psychoanalytic Mystic*. London: Free Association Books.

Eigen, M. (1999). *Toxic Nourishment*. London: Karnac.

Eigen, M. (2001a). *Ecstasy*. Middletown, CT: Wesleyan University Press.

Eigen, M. (2001b). *Damaged Bonds*. London: Karnac.

Eigen, M. (2002). *Rage*. Middletown, CT: Wesleyan University Press.

Eigen, M. (2004a). *The Psychotic Core*. London: Karnac.

Eigen, M. (2004b). *The Electrified Tightrope*, A Phillips (Ed.). London: Karnac.

Eigen, M. (2004c). *Psychic Deadness*. London: Karnac.

Eigen, M. (2004d). *The Sensitive Self*. Middletown, CT: Wesleyan University Press.

Eigen, M. (2006a). *Age of Psychopathy*. Available at: www.psychoanalysis-and-therapy.com/human_nature/eigen/pref.html

Eigen, M. (2006b). *Lust*. Middletown, CT: Wesleyan University Press.

Eigen, M. (2006c). *Feeling Matters*. London: Karnac.

Eigen, M. (2007). Guilt in an age of psychopathy. *Psychoanalytic Review, 88*: 455–481.

Eigen, M. (2008). Hallucination and psychopathy. *International Forum of Psychoanalysis, 17*: 4–15.

Eigen, M. (2011). *Contact With the Depths*. London: Karnac.

Eigen, M. (2012). *Kabbalah and Psychoanalysis*. London: Karnac.

Eigen, M. (2013). *Reshaping the Self*. London: Karnac.

Eigen, M. (2014a). *A Felt Sense: More Explorations of Psychoanalysis and Kabbalah*. London: Karnac.

Eigen, M. (2014b). *The Birth of Experience*. London: Karnac.

Eigen, M. (2014c). *Faith*. London: Karnac.

Eigen, M., & Govrin, A. (2007). *Conversations With Michael Eigen*. London: Karnac.

Elkin, H. (1972). On selfhood and the development of ego structures in infancy. *Psychoanalytic Review, 59*: 389–416.

Espy, J. C. (2015). *There is No Body: A Journey through the Dark Boroughs of a Pedophilic Cannibal's Mind. Volume 3*. London: Karnac.
Freud, S. (1900a). *The Interpretation of Dreams. S. E.*, 4–5. London: Hogarth.
Freud, S. (1918b). *From the History of an Infantile Neurosis. S. E.*, 17: 1–122. London: Hogarth.
Ghiselin, B. (1952). *The Creative Process*. Oakland, CA: University of California Press.
Jung, C. G. (1989). *Memories, Dreams, Reflections*, A. Jaffe (Ed.), C. Winston & R. Winston (Trans.). New York: Vintage Books.
Kohler, W. (1976). *The Mentality of Apes*. New York: Liveright.
Kohut, H. (1971). *The Analysis of the Self*. Chicago, IL: University of Chicago Press.
Lacan, J. (1981). *The Four Fundamental Concepts of Psycho-Analysis*, J.-A. Miller (Ed.), A. Sheridan (Trans.). New York: W. W. Norton.
Lacan, J. (2006). *Écrits: The First Complete Edition in English*, B. Fink (Trans.). New York: W. W. Norton.
Langer, S. (1941). *Philosophy in a New Key: A Study in the Symbolism of Reason, Rite, and Art*. London: Pelican.
Levinas, E. (1969). *Totality and Infinity*, A. Lingis (Trans.). Pittsburgh, PA: Duquesne University Press.
Levinas, E. (1987). *Time and the Other*, R. A. Cohen (Trans.). Pittsburgh, PA: Duquesne University Press.
Liebes, Y. (1993). *Studies in the Zohar*. Albany, NY: State University of New York Press.
Matt, D. C. (1998). *God and the Big Bang*. Woodstock, VT: Jewish Lights.
Matt, D. C. (2004). *The Zohar* (Pritzger Edition). Stanford, CA: Stanford University Press.
Matt, D. C. (2009). *Zohar: Annotated and Explained*. Woodstock, VT: Skylight Paths.
Meltzer, D. (2008). *Sexual States of Mind*. London: Karnac.
Merleau-Ponty, M. (2013/1945). *Phenomenology of Perception*, D. Landes (Trans.). London: Routledge, 2013.
Milner, M. (1987). *The Suppressed Madness of Sane Men: Forty-Four Years of Exploring Psychoanalysis*. London: Routledge.
Miller, I., & Souter, K. (2013). *Beckett and Bion: The (Im)Patient Voice in Psychotherapy and Literature*. London: Karnac.
Read, H. (1965). *Icon and Idea: The Function of Art in the Development of Human Consciousness*. New York: Schocken.
Schneerson, M. M. (1998). *On the Essence of Chassidus*. Brooklyn, NY: Kehot Publication Society.

Steinsaltz, A. (2006). *The Thirteen Petalled Rose: A Discourse on the Essence of Jewish Existence and Belief.* New York: Basic Books.
Suzuki, D. T. (1932). *Lankavatara Sutra.* London: Routledge.
Tausk, V. (1933). On the origin of the 'influencing machine' in schizophrenia, D. Feigenbaum (Trans.). *Psychoanalytic Quarterly, 2*: 519–556.
Teitelbaum, S. (2016). Do I have to draw you a picture? Sigmund Freud, imagery, and the Wolfman's drawing. *Psychoanalytic Inquiry, 36*: 633–643.
Winnicott, D. W. (1982). *Playing and Reality.* London: Routledge.
Winnicott, D. W. (1992). *Psycho-Analytic Explorations,* C. Winnicott, R. Shepherd, & M. Davis (Eds.). Cambridge, MA: Harvard University Press.

INDEX

abuse, 13, 98
  child, 78–79, 113
  financial, 15
  mental, 15
  sexual, 15
affect(ive), 38, 62, 121
  attitude, x, 22, 34–35, 44, 75, 130
  context, 5
  deprivation, 122
  images, xiv
  imagination, xiii–xiv
  intensity, 122
  life, 121
  worlds, 121
aggression, 4, 15–17, 21, 23, 73, 77–78, 126
  force, ix
  impulses, 4
anxiety, 58, 72, 99, 102, 118, 128
  abandonment, 72
  birth, 58, 72
  castration, 72
  catastrophic, 57

creativity, 110
death, 58
dire, 22
life, 58
psychotic, 11, 42, 79, 130–131
Arendt, H., 62
Arieti, S., xv, 124

Berdyaev, N., 27, 51
Bergson, H., 27
Bettelheim, B., xv, 124
Bion, F., 69
Bion, W. R.
  alpha function, 28
  Big Bang, 61
  cited works, 2, 19, 23, 27–30, 41, 44, 50, 60, 69, 72, 102, 122–123, 132
  grid
    F, 73
    O, xii, 29, 59, 66, 73, 132
    T, 73
birth, 37–38, 44–45, 51–52, 57–61, 64
  see also: anxiety

failed, 58, 67
incomplete, 58
murders, 44
of experience, 64
process, 37, 45, 58
psychological, xii, 37
still-, 55, 64
therapy, 37, 44
Blake, W., x, 6, 26–27, 38, 61
Bloom, H., 52, 71
Bonaparte, M., 121

case studies
 Denise, xiii, 93–104
 Devi, 83–84
 Don, 125–126
 Garren, 85–86
 Gerry, xiv, 107–112, 114–116, 118
 Harris, 30–32
 Lou, xiv, 100–105
 Marin, 81–83
 Norm, 93–97, 99–100, 104
 Stu, 89–91
Chuang Tzu, 65
Cleckley, H. M., 19
conscious(ness), 1, 6, 60–61, 65, 102,
  129–130 *see also*: unconscious
 control, 53
 pre-, 129
 self-, 60

Daws, L., 121
development(al), xiv, 40, 53, 60, 74
 failure, 2

Eddington, A. S., 59, 65
ego, 4, 8, 13–14
 body, 135
 -centric, 12, 16
 control, 27
 -mania, 22
 mental, 135
 strength, 122
Eigen, M., 13, 16–17, 25–29, 32, 34–35,
  50, 53, 57–62, 64–69, 73, 75, 78,
  101, 122–123

Elkin, H., xv, 11, 16–18, 61, 121, 123
emptiness, 5, 29–30, 66
 –fullness, 29, 122
 –plenitude, 122
 pregnant, 29, 59
Espy, J. C., 13

fantasy, 17, 22, 38, 95–98
 bliss, 94
 gratification, xiii
 hallucinatory, 7
 script, 12
 sex, 96
Freud, S., ix–x, xv, 1–2, 4, 6–7, 12–17,
  19–20, 22, 26, 38–41, 43, 52–53,
  55–58, 64–65, 71–73, 78, 109,
  116–117, 121–123, 125, 128–129,
  133–134
frustration, 1–2, 5, 16, 53, 79, 96
 awareness of, 3
 evasion, 3–4
 gratification–, xiii
 modification, 3, 5
 total, 1

Ghiselin, B., 29, 53
Govrin, A., 73
guilt, 14, 16–17, 20, 72

hallucination, 2, 5–9, 22, 28, 57, 79
hate, 96, 101, 115
 love–, 34
 objects, 7
 self-, xv, 22, 109, 115, 125
Hunt, H., 19, 43

Jung, C. G., xv, 22, 27, 33–34, 39, 43,
  51, 109, 121, 123

Kabbalah, 34, 39, 42, 66
 Ein Sof, 66
 Lurianic, 68
 Tree of Life, 25, 44
Kohler, W., 53
Kohut, H., 27
Kris, E., 121

Lacan, J., xv, 27, 38, 123
Langer, S., 27
Levinas, E., x, 8–9
Liebes, Y., 67

Matt, D. C., 60, 64, 67
Meltzer, D., 62
Merleau-Ponty, M., 26
Miller, A., 12
Miller, I., 51
Milner, M., 29, 40, 59

object, 7, 57 *see also*: hate
　lost, 18
　love, 7
　physical, 65

rage, 5, 9, 16, 67, 78, 98, 121, 134–135
　parental, 101
Read, H., 28
reality, xv, 6–8, 23, 27, 55, 62, 66, 78, 97, 114, 133
　elusive, 68
　emotional, 29, 41, 59, 72–73, 78, 127–128
　fundamental, 66, 132
　imaginative, 8
　infinite, 132
　living, 73
　of identity, 63
　outer, 30
　principle, 4–5
　psychic, 39, 64, 73, 78
　psychical, 75, 132
　ultimate, xii, 29, 59
　unknown, 66, 73

schizophrenia, 11, 16, 19, 43, 115
　chronic, 77
　paranoid, 55
Schneerson, M. M., 29
self *see also*: conscious, hate
　-affirmation, 44
　-aggrandizement, 21
　-assertion, 15–16, 44
　-assurance, 21
　-attack, 20
　-care, 105
　-celebratory, 74
　-centered, 16
　-confinement, 55
　-confusing, 69
　-contact, 41
　-creation, 41
　-debasement, 126
　-defense, 17
　-denigration, 125
　destruction of, 19
　evolution of, 2
　-experience, 67
　false, 19
　fecal, xv, 125
　-giving, 18
　-idealization, 21
　-idolatry, 74
　-image, 35
　-inflation, 21
　-injury, 54, 105
　-interest, 12, 78
　-introduction, 34, 132
　loss of, 61
　-love, 22, 98
　-maintenance, 77
　–other, 16, 71
　-pity, 101
　-preservation, 54
　-protectiveness, 5
　-reliance, 18
　-righteousness, 18, 79, 131
　-sacrifice, 15
　-transcendence, 44, 60
sexual(ity), 3–4, 7, 15, 125 *see also*: abuse, fantasy
　counterpart, 95
　impotence, 52
　instincts, 4
　intercourse, 60
　interest, 108
　organs, 62
Souter, K., 51
Steinsaltz, A., 64
Suzuki, D. T., 29

Tausk, V., 13
Teitelbaum, S., 123
Trump, D., xi, 20–22

unconscious(ness), 1, 6, 38, 98–99, 104, 110, 133 *see also*: conscious
  being, 1
  life, 26
  processes, 129
  sense, 5, 99

violence, x, 6, 18, 44, 78–80

war, x, 4, 15–16, 18, 27, 60–61, 64, 72, 75, 78, 80, 101, 132
  civil, 15
  cold, 79, 131
  First World, 20
  Iraq, 11–12
  parochial, 72
  Second World, 13, 18
  therapy, 38–39
  threat of, 13
Winnicott, D. W., xv, 17–19, 28, 37, 40, 52, 58, 82, 122–124